Educating African American Students

Foundations, Curriculum, and Experiences

Edited by
Abul Pitre, Esrom Pitre, Ruth Ray,
and Twana Hilton-Pitre

Rowman & Littlefield Education
A division of
ROWMAN & LITTLEFIELD PUBLISHERS, INC.
Lanham • New York • Toronto • Plymouth, UK

Published by Rowman & Littlefield Education
A division of Rowman & Littlefield Publishers, Inc.
A wholly owned subsidary of The Rowman & Littlefield Publishing Group,
Inc.
4501 Forbes Boulevard, Suite 200, Lanham, Maryland 20706
http://www.rowmaneducation.com

Estover Road, Plymouth PL6 7PY, United Kingdom

British Library Cataloguing in Publication Information Available

Library of Congress Cataloging-in-Publication Data

Educating African American students : foundations, curriculum, and
experiences / edited by Abul Pitre ... [et al.].
        p. cm. — (Critical black pedagogy in education)
   ISBN 978-1-60709-232-2 (cloth : alk. paper) — ISBN 978-1-60709-233-9
(pbk. : alk. paper) — ISBN 978-1-60709-234-6 (electronic)
   1. African American students—Education. 2. African American boys—
Education. I. Pitre, Abul.
   LC2771.E25 2009
   371.829'96073—dc22   2009012015

∞™ The paper used in this publication meets the minimum requirements of
American National Standard for Information Sciences—Permanence of
Paper for Printed Library Materials, ANSI/NISO Z39.48-1992.

Printed in the United States of America.

Contents

Series Foreword

Historically the state of black education has been at the center of American life. When the first blacks arrived to the Americas to be made slaves, a process of *mis-education* was systematized into the very fabric of American life. The newly arrived blacks were dehumanized and forced through a process that was described by a conspicuous slave owner named Willie Lynch as a "breaking process": "Hence the horse and the nigger must be broken; that is, break them from one form of mental life to another—keep the body and take the mind" (Hassan-EL, 2007, p. 14). This horrendous process of breaking the African from one form of mental life into another included an elaborate educational system that was designed to put to death the creative black mind. Elijah Muhammad called this a process that made black people blind, deaf, and dumb—meaning the minds of black people were taken from them. He proclaimed, "Back when our fathers were brought here and put into slavery 400 years ago, 300 [of] which they served as servitude slaves, they taught our people everything against themselves" (Pitre, 2008, p. 6). Woodson similarly decried, "Even schools for Negroes, then, are places where they must be convinced of their inferiority. The thought of inferiority of the Negro is drilled into him in almost every class he enters and almost in every book he studies" (p. 2).

Today the issue of black education seems to be at a crossroads. With the passing of the No Child Left Behind Act of 2001, schools that serve a large majority of black children have been under the scrutiny of politicians who vigilantly proclaim the need to improve schools while not realizing that these schools were never intended to educate or educe the divine powers within black people. Watkins (2001) posits that after the Civil War, schools for black people—particularly those in the South—were designed by wealthy philanthropists. These philanthropists designed "seventy-five years of education for blacks" (pp. 41–42). Seventy-five years from 1865 brings us to 1940, and today we are sixty-nine years removed from 1940. These numbers do not add up to equal the seventy-five years of scripted education; to truly understand the plight of black education one has to consider the historical impact of seventy-five years of scripted education and its influence on the present state of black education. Presently, schools are still controlled by ruling class whites who hold major power. Woodson (2008) saw this as a problem in his day and argued, "The education of the Negroes, then, the most important thing in the uplift of Negroes, is almost entirely in the hands of those who have enslaved them and now segregate them" (p. 22). Here, Woodson cogently argues for historical understanding:

> To point out merely the defects as they appear today will be of little benefit to the present and future generations. These things must be viewed in their historic setting. The conditions of today have been determined by what has taken place in the past. (p. 9)

Watkins (2001) summarizes that the "white architects of black education . . . carefully selected and sponsored knowledge, which contributed to obedience, subservience, and political docility" (p. 40). Historical knowledge is essential to understanding the plight of black education.

A major historical point in black education was the famous *Brown v. the Board of Education of Topeka, Kansas*, in which the Supreme Court ruled that segregation deprived blacks of equality of education. Thus, schools were ordered to integrate with all deliberate speed. This historic ruling has continued to impact the education of black children in myriad and complex ways.

To date, the famous landmark case of *Brown v. the Board of Education of Topeka, Kansas*, has not lived up to the paper that it was printed on. Schools are more segregated today than they were at the time of the *Brown* decision. Even more disheartening is that schools that are supposedly desegregated may have tracking programs, such as "gifted and talented," that attract white students and give schools the appearance of being integrated while actually creating segregation within the school. Spring (2006) calls this "second-generation segregation" and asserts:

> Unlike segregation that existed by state laws in the South before the 1954 *Brown* decision, second generation forms of segregation can occur in schools with balanced racial populations; for instance, all White students may be placed in one academic track and all African American or Hispanic students in another track. (p. 82)

In this type of setting, white supremacy may become rooted in the subconscious minds of both black and white students. Nieto and Bode (2008) highlight the internalized damage that tracking may have on students when they say students "may begin to believe that their placement in these groups is natural and a true reflection of whether they are 'smart,' 'average,' or 'dumb'" (p. 119). According to Oakes and Lipton (2007), "African American and Latino students are assigned to low-track classes more often than White (and Asian) students, leading to two separate schools in one building—one white and one minority" (p. 308). Nieto and Bode (2008) argue the teaching strategy in segregated settings "leaves its mark on pedagogy as well. Students in the lowest levels are most likely to be subjected to rote memorization and static teaching methods" (p. 119). These findings are consistent with Lipman's findings (1998): "Scholars have argued that desegregation policy has been framed by what is in the interest of whites, has abstracted from excellence in education, and has been constructed as racial integration, thus avoiding the central problem of institutional racism" (p. 11). Hammond (2005) is not alone, then, in observing that "the school experiences of African American and other minority students in the United States continue to be substantially, separate and unequal" (p. 202).

Clearly, the education of black students must be addressed with a sense of urgency like never before. Lipman (1998) alludes to the crisis of black education, noting that "the overwhelming failure of schools to develop the talents and potentials of students of color is a national crisis" (p. 2). In just about every negative category in education, black children are overrepresented. Again Lipman (1998) alludes, "The character and depth of the crisis are only dimly depicted by low achievement scores and high rates of school failure and dropping out" (p. 2). Under the disguise of raising student achievement, the No Child Left Behind Act has instead contributed to the demise of educational equality for black students. Hammond (2004) cites the negative impact of the law: "The Harvard Civil Rights Project, along with other advocacy groups, has warned that the law threatens to increase the growing dropout rate and pushout rates for students of color, ultimately reducing access to education for these students rather than enhancing it" (p. 4). Asante (2005) summarizes the crisis of black education when he says, "I cannot honestly say that I have ever found a school in the United States run by whites that adequately prepares black children to enter the world as sane human beings . . . an exploitative, capitalist system that enshrines plantation owners as saints and national heroes cannot possibly create sane black children" (p. 65). The issues surrounding the education of black students are indeed a national crisis that must be put at the forefront of the African American agenda for liberation.

In this series, *Critical Black Pedagogy in Education*, I call upon a wide range of scholars, educators, and activists to speak to the issues of educating black students. The series is designed to not only highlight issues that may negatively impact the education of black students, but also to provide possibilities for improving the quality of education for black students. Another major goal of the series is to help pre-service teachers, practicing teachers, administrators, school board members, and those concerned with the plight of black education by providing a wide range of scholarly research that is thought provoking and stimulating. The series will cover every imaginable aspect of black education from K–12 schools to higher education. It is hoped that this series will generate deep reflection and stimulate action-praxis to uproot the social injustices that exist in schools that serve large numbers of black students.

In the past, significant scholarly research has been conducted on the education of black students; however, there does not seem to be a coherent theoretical approach to addressing the education of black students that is outside of European dominance. Thus, the series will serve as a foundation for what I call *Critical Black Pedagogy in Education*— an examination of black leaders, scholars, activists, and their exegeses and challenge of power relations in black education. The idea is based on the educational ideas of Elijah Muhammad, Carter G. Woodson, and others whose leadership and ideas could transform schools for black students. One can only imagine how schools would look if Elijah Muhammad, Carter G. Woodson, Marcus Garvey, or other significant black leaders were in charge. Additionally, the election of President Barack Hussein Obama as the first black president of the United States of America offers us a compelling examination of transformative leadership that could be inculcated into America's schools. The newly elected president's history of working for social justice and his campaign theme based on Change We Can Believe In, along with his inaugural address that challenged America to embrace a new era is similar to the ideas embodied in *Critical Black Pedagogy in Education*.

Critical Black Pedagogy in Education is a call to develop an entirely new educational system. This new system must envision how black leaders would transform schools within the context of the diversity in society. With this in mind, we are not only looking historically at black leaders but we also are looking at contemporary extensions of these great leaders. Karen Johnson (in press) describes its necessity: "There is a need for researchers, educators, policy makers, etc. to comprehend the emancipatory teaching practices that African American teachers employed that in turn contributed to academic success of Black students as well as offered a vision for a more just society." Freire (2000) also lays a foundation for critical black pedagogy in education by declaring, "It would be a contradiction in terms if the oppressors not only defended but actually implemented a liberating education" (p. 54). Thus, critical black pedagogy in education is a historical and contemporary examination of black leaders (scholars, ministers, educators, politicians, etc.) who challenged the European dominance of black education and suggested ideas for the education of black people.

Educating African American Students: Foundations, Curriculum, and Experiences is the first offering in this series, and it examines some of the historical issues surrounding black education, curriculum issues, and the experiences of African American students. The book is a compilation of essays and empirical research studies that allow the reader to juxtapose the theoretical with the practical. The contributors of this book glean from theoretical approaches found in critical theory, multicultural education, and the Afrocentric idea.

The book is a welcome addition to the literature on black education. Similar to Joyce King's (2005) *Black Education: A Transformative Research and Action Agenda for the New Century*, this book addresses research issues raised in *The Commission on Research in Black Education* (CORIBE). Like CORIBE's agenda, *Educating African American Students* focuses on "using culture as an asset in the design of learning environments that are applicable to students' lives and that lead students toward more analytical and critical learning" (p. 353). The book examines the experiences of black students and offers unique insight about how those experiences can be transferred to the practice of social justice in schools. The book is indeed provocative, compelling, and rich with information that will move those concerned with equity, justice, and equality of education to a renewed activism.

Abul Pitre
Series Editor

REFERENCES

Asante, K. (2005). *Race, rhetoric, & identity: The architecton of soul.* Amherst, NY: Humanity Books.

Freire, P. (2000). *Pedagogy of the oppressed.* New York: Continuum.

Hammond-Darling, L. (2004). From "separate but equal" to "no child left behind": The collision of new standards and old inequalities. In D. Meier and G. Wood (Eds.), *Many children left behind: How the no child left behind act is damaging our children and our schools* (pp. 3–32). Boston: Beacon Press.

———. (2005). New standards and old inequalities: School reform and the education of African American students. In J. King (Ed.), *Black education: A transformative research and action agenda for the new century* (pp. 197–224). Mahwah, NJ: Lawrence Earlbaum Associates.

Hassan-EL, K. (2007). *The Willie Lynch letter and the making of slaves.* Besenville, IL: Lushena Books.

Johnson, K. and Pitre, A. (Eds.). (in press). *African American women educators: A critical examination of their pedagogies, educational ideas, and activism from the nineteenth to the mid-twentieth centuries.* Lanham, MD: University Press of America.

King, J. E. (Ed.). (2005). *Black education: A transformative research and action agenda for the new century.* Mahwah, NJ: Lawrence Erlbaum Associates.

Lipman, P. (1998). *Race and the restructuring of school*. Albany, NY: SUNY Press.

Nieto, S., and Bode, P. (2008). *Affirming diversity: The sociopolitical context of multicultural education* (5th ed.) Boston, MA: Allyn & Bacon.

Oakes, J., and Lipton, M. (2007). *Teaching to change the world* (3rd ed.). Boston: McGraw Hill.

Pitre, A. (2008). *The education philosophy of Elijah Muhammad: Education for a new world* (2nd ed.). Lanham, MD: University Press of America.

Spring, J. (2006). *American education*. New York: McGraw Hill.

Watkins, W. (2001). *The white architects of black education: Ideology and power in America 1865–1954*. New York: Teachers College Press.

Woodson, C. G. (2008). *The mis-education of the Negro*. Drewryville, VA: Kha Books.

Foreword

It has been fifty-five years since the U.S. Supreme Court rendered the *Brown v. Board of Education of Topeka, Kansas*, decision, which ruled that it was unconstitutional to maintain racially segregated schools in the United States. The 1954 decision remains among one of the most significant judicial rulings in U.S. history. Despite the continued slow pace to desegregate schools "with all deliberate speed," Brown set an important moral and legal standard for human rights activism both in the United States and abroad. Yet fifty-five years later many African Americans are still struggling to ensure that equal educational opportunities are offered to all citizens.

I am privileged at this historical moment in time to have the opportunity to write a foreword for *Educating African American Students: Foundations, Curriculum, and Experiences*, edited by Abul Pitre, Esrom Pitre, Ruth Ray, and Twana Hilton-Pitre. The book addresses some of today's most urgent educational issues facing African American students—from historical analysis of black education to counseling African American girls in a white-school setting. These dynamic authors provide the readers with unique insight about how African American student experiences can be transformed to the practice of social justice in schools. The future of African American students depends on how quickly we can end the educational inequalities that exist between African American students and other students from diverse backgrounds. Research shows that the current No Child Left Behind (NCLB) Act of 2001 may be causing achievement gaps to widen rather than close. The NCLB policy, which is narrowly focused on standardization and assessment, neglects issues of access to high-quality education and curriculum taught by competent and caring teachers who hold high expectations for African American students.

Educating African American Students: Foundations, Curriculum, and Experiences highlights essential issues such as critical theory, multicultural education, the impact of desegregation, the overrepresentation of African American males in special education, the experiences of African American males in urban schools, and the Afro-centric idea. Each contributing author provides unique research findings and solutions that holds particular significance for the nation's teachers, educational leaders, and policymakers. The information provided in this book offers freshness and encouraging hope for educating African American students.

Dr. Terence Hicks
Fayetteville State University

Acknowledgments

I am grateful to my new colleagues at Fayetteville State University who have made the transition to the university and its surrounding community a pleasurable experience. The support received from Dr. Leontye Lewis, Dean of the College of Education; Dr. Terence Hicks, Educational Leadership Department Chair; Dr. Joseph Johnson, Educational Leadership Professor; Dr. Frederick Smith, Educational Leadership Professor; Dr. Linda Wilson-Jones, Director of the Doctoral Program in Educational Leadership; and Mrs. Mable Hawkins, Administrative Support has afforded me the opportunity to complete this project in a timely manner. I am also indebted to Patti Belcher, editor at Rowman & Littlefield for her guidance, support, and suggestions and her ability to see the project to fruition. Of course I could never forget my colleagues at Southern University—Dr. Frank Cook, Dr. Luria Stubblefield, Dr. Katina January, Dr. Huey Perry, Dr. Charles Bryant, Dr. Carol McCree, and Dr. Roy Jacobs—who have inspired, encouraged, and motivated me to think more deeply about my future in academia.

I am most grateful for my wife, Ruby, who has always been a source of support and consolation since we first met. To my children Ajah, Alaiah, and our newborn Alijah: you make the fight for equality of education even nearer to my heart.

Abul Pitre
February 2009

Introduction

The Culture of Death

The African American Child and Schooling

ABUL PITRE, FRANK COOK, AND CAROL MCCREE

The culture of death has taken over the lives of too many African American youths. On a daily basis the white-controlled media outlets bombard African American youth with negative self images. These media images depict African American youth as gang bangers, drug dealers, misogynists, and gold-wearing criminal misfits. African American youth are internalizing these negative images, causing too many to develop a self identity rooted in the media constructed images. Kincheloe and Hayes (2007) give an excellent example of the self-internalization encountered by African American students with the example of Tre, one of his African American students:

> I have heard it a hundred times, "don't mess with Tre, he's a bad mother fucker."
> "Did you hear about Tre?" one student asks his classmates.
> "No, what did he do this time?' they respond.
> "That crazy Tre beat Rasheed Parker and Don Kincade half to death."
> "Wow, he's a bad mother fucker," the classmates respond in unison.
> (p. 26)

Kincheloe and Hayes (2007) articulate the psychological impact of these negative media images:

> As I listen to such conversations, I understand that Tre and all the other kids who fit in the category in question are eliciting awe, fear, and, most importantly, respect from their classmates. In addition to gaining a higher status persona in his peer group, Tre has internalized

a prevalent stereotype of black violence, advanced so successfully by T.V. and movies. (p. 26)

War has been declared on African American youth by the cultural engineers who have designed, shaped, and constructed a culture of death for them. These cultural engineers, who are wise and skillful scientists, are using silent weapons of mass destruction aimed at destroying the minds of African American youth. The problem therefore lies in overcoming the culture of death to construct a culture of life through the schooling process.

Culture is used here as those social or intragroup behaviors that have been institutionalized by law or custom. Carter G. Woodson seems to have such in mind with his classic book *The Mis-education of the Negro,* in which he discusses the role of schooling in mis-educating African Americans, thus creating a culture opposite of life. Culture binds a people together. It prescribes behaviors and foundational communities such as family, marriage, language, music, art, religion, food choices, and so on. Through structured institutionalized arrangements, communities pass on ideas, beliefs, and ways of seeing the world to each successive generation. African American youth, through a process of schooling, are not being taught how to overcome the prescribed culture of death.

Once in school, African American children are taught to see the world from the eyes of those in the dominant group. Through high stakes testing, the culture of death is multiplied as the real problems that face African American youth are ignored. The primary emphasis in too many public schools that serve African Americans is being placed on skills and testing as a replacement for education. African American children are being negatively impacted to a much greater degree than their white peers. Furthermore, mis-education is being replaced with no education, which can be seen in the expulsions, dropout rates, and illiteracy rates of African American students (Lipman, 1998). The schools and the curricula are completely out of touch with the reality of African American students.

Once again the significance of power and authority come into play regarding decisions about what gets put in the curriculum, whose knowledge will prevail, and for what purpose. Critical pedagogists question the relationship between knowledge and power, arguing that knowledge is contested political terrain (Freire, 2000; McLaren, 2007; Kincheloe and Hayes, 2007). Carter G. Woodson and Elijah Muhammad argued similarly that the education of African Americans was controlled by white people in positions of power. Elijah Muhammad (1965) clearly described this phenomena when he said, "We have been to the schools of our slave-master's children. We have been to their schools and gone as far as they allowed us to go" (p. 34). Asa Hilliard (2001) decried, "We do not control the institutions that educate and socialize our children: the schools, the mass media, the law, etc." (p. 106). Today not much has changed with regard to the white-controlled education of African Americans. Those in positions of real power have continued to maintain an educational system that keeps African Americans from reaching their full potential.

African Americans have historically been culturally dominated by Anglicized white America like some other ethnic groups, notably Native Americans and Hispanics (Spring, 2006). The significant difference is that other groups were not enslaved and were not forced to lose their names, culture, religion, and God; this was the lot of the Africans. While not all Africans were of the same ethnicity any more than all Europeans were of the same heritage, the early Africans faced cultural dilemmas. First, their new environment provided no cultural affirmation; second, they were forced to forget the culture of their ancestors; and third, they were forced to adapt to a culture that was not rooted in their being. This was not *benign* but *malignant neglect* and the malignancy continues into the twenty-first century.

Movies featuring characters such as the feuding cowboy and Indian or Tarzan exemplified the "white is right" mentality. On television, Tarzan could yell and spread fear into hundreds of Africans while African American viewers clapped their hands in support. African Americans did not know their history because they had been Americanized and were not in tune with reality; thus, they could cheer for images that reflected the power of their oppressors. Today's African American youths are even more distant from their roots. Not only are they ever distant, but African American educators are suffering from historical amnesia. In schools, this lack of historical discourse has rendered African American youth culturally dead, leaving too many unknowledgeable of self, uncaring, and without a foundation for making cultural and historical decisions—in a word, *lost*.

The root problem lies in the fact that American education was designed to transmit the cultural heritage of those in the dominant group. The Anglicized heritage, traditions, values, and myths of England and America were constants. The key socializing institutions were the school, home, and church. These institutions were supported by laws and customs forcing Natives and Africans to become Anglicized and they lost their cultural identity in the process. Banks (2008) argues, "Some individuals of color in the United States—such as many African Americans, Native Americans, Puerto Rican Americans—in their effort to assimilate and to participate fully in mainstream institutions, become very Anglo-Saxon in their ways of viewing the world and in their behavior" (p. 3). As a result, there is a need for accurate school curricula that is as diverse as the people of America. There is also a need to restore and awaken the consciousness of so-called minorities, especially African Americans and Native Americans. The culture of death that is prevalent among too many African American youths must be replaced with a culture of life. This must be done through a schooling process that educates or brings forth the genetic powers dormant in African American youth.

Using a combination of essays and empirical studies, the contributors of this timely book highlight in its pages some of the significant issues and experiences faced in the education of African American students. Drawing from critical pedagogy, several of the authors critique the education of African American students with regard to the foundations of education, the curriculum, and the experiences encountered by African American students.

In the first section, *Foundations*, Rodrick Jenkins captures the historical role of black education with a particular emphasis on desegregation in Louisiana, arguing that desegregation does not equate to progress for African Americans. Next, world-renowned psychologist Naim Akbar discusses the No Child Left Behind Act and its claim to eradicate educational disparities that exist in the education of African Americans. Dr. Akbar argues that the education of African Americans must be examined in a sociopolitical context. The *Foundations* section concludes with Abul Pitre illuminating the need for knowledge of self with the argument that achievement must be redefined and reworked from the perspective of African Americans.

The second section, *Curriculum*, examines some of the issues that African Americans face within the curriculum. Rodrick Jenkins analyzes the social studies curriculum in relation to African American students using Freire's ideas of banking education as a lens through which to view the method of educating African American students in social studies. In addition, he summarizes how the current social studies curriculum in Louisiana portrays African Americans as voiceless and inactive agents for social change. Shahid Muhammad confronts the issue of mathematics and African American students, detailing the problems, dilemmas, and fears faced by African American students when learning mathematics and offering advice on how to address these issues. Esrom Pitre concludes this section with the examination of a nationwide problem: the overrepresentation of African American males in special education. Pitre highlights some of the major factors that contribute to the overrepresentation of African American males in special education and argues that special education has served as a loophole for schools trying to resist desegregation.

The *Experiences* section includes empirical studies that examine the experiences of African American students in school. In their article, Michelle Barconey and Abul Pitre discuss the historical role of education, teacher ideologies, and Frerian concepts related to the education of African American males, using African American male student comments regarding their experiences in an urban school to accentuate their analysis. In the subsequent chapter, Professors Esrom Pitre and Chance Lewis interview African American males and relay chilling stories of these students' experiences in special education. Next is a study by Professors Abul Pitre, Ruth Ray, and Luria Stubblefield regarding the challenge of implementing black history into school curricula. Their article highlights the controversy surrounding a black history program that broke from tradition and the impact of this experience on the lives of African American student leaders.

Following this, Peter Sheppard devotes a chapter on high-achieving African American mathematic students in underperforming schools. This chapter gives insight about the role of teachers in providing African American students with the motivation and inspiration to be successful. The *Experiences* section concludes with Twana Hilton-Pitre's insightful study of African American females in all-white school setting. The chapter examines a plethora of issues faced by African American females, such as racism and oppression, in the white school setting and concludes with a very powerful counseling strategy that could be used to overcome the negative schooling experiences of African American females in all-white school settings. The article also has significant implications for African American males.

The education of the African American youth is at a major crossroad in American history. The failing U.S. economy, the destruction of the African American family, the drug influx, the media, and the constructed images of African American youth along with the schooling process have created a culture of death among too many African American youths. Additionally, the No Child Left Behind Act (NCLB) has suffocated any critical classroom discourse that could liberate the group. McLaren (2007) correctly argues that schools and teachers have been reduced to technicians or what Freire refers to as "things." NCLB has done exactly what we believe its architects intended from the onset, which was to dehumanize mass numbers of students. Gabbard and Ross (2004) argue, "Moreever, the "responsible men" drafted NCLB to ensure that public schools will fail" (p.41). African American students have become the victims of this slave-making process. History has shown that the education of African Americans was designed for the benefit of the white ruling powers. In this book, the contributors hope to provide information that will propel us to challenge the unjust schooling practices that impact African American youth. By providing both a critical analysis and a positive praxis, this book can give those concerned with the education of African American youth a sense of hope that collectively, we have the power to change the negative circumstances around the education of African American youth.

REFERENCES

Banks, J. (2008). *An introduction to multicultural education* (4th ed.). Boston: Allyn & Bacon.
Freire, P. (2000). *Pedagogy of the oppressed.* New York: Continuum.

Gabbard, D., and Ross, E. (2004). *Defending public schools: Education under the security state*. Westport, CT. Greenwood Publishing Group.

Hilliard, A. (2001). *The maroon within us: Selected essays on African American community socialization*. Baltimore: Black Classic Press.

Kincheloe, J., and Hayes, K. (2007). *Teaching city kids: Understanding and appreciating them*. New York: Peter Lang Publishing.

Lipman, P. (1998). *Race, class, and power in school restructuring*. Albany: SUNY Press.

McLaren, P. (2007). *Life in schools: An introduction to critical pedagogy in the foundations of education* (5th ed.). Boston: Allyn & Bacon.

Muhammad, E. (1965). *Message to the blackman in America*. Chicago: Final Call.

Spring, J. (2006). *American education*. New York: McGraw Hill.

Woodson, C. G. (2008). *The mis-education of the Negro*. Drewryville, VA: Kha Books.

Part I

FOUNDATIONS

CHAPTER 1

A Historical Analysis of Black Education

The Impact of Desegregation on African Americans

RODRICK JENKINS

INTRODUCTION

This chapter examines faculty desegregation policies and their implications regarding curriculum for African American students. The most fitting way to introduce the problem is with a statement made in 1968 by J. K. Haynes, executive secretary of the Louisiana Education Association (LEA), which was Louisiana's black educators' association during segregation. At the time, LEA represented 15,000 mostly black educators. Concerning the desegregation policies of closing black schools and the dismissal or demotion of black educators, a 1968 *Baton Rouge Advocate* article quotes Haynes as predicting that "in the absence of this institution [the black school] and the black educator, there is created a *void* in the black community and as a consequence, the black youngsters will be emasculated of all motivation, aspiration and hope . . . black education suffers a loss and the real violence is done to the black community" (*Baton Rouge Advocate*, 1968). This article forces one to question the notion that desegregation equates to progress for African Americans.

During Jim Crow, the fact that African American educators controlled the education of black children at the school level constituted a source of power. It provided an opportunity for the black community to deflect racist curriculum policies aimed at black children and at the same time offered black educators the opportunity to implement more relevant curricular ideas. Alvis Adair (1984) reached a similar conclusion in an earlier critique of desegregation:

> The many landmark court decisions in civil rights cases are examples of assaults upon this white stronghold. Yet this White power empire remains fully intact. In fact, their power has now been strengthened in the educational system as a result of the extension of their direct control over the management and administration of public education for Blacks at the school building and classroom levels. This supplantation was the direct consequence of the desegregation movement, which has been one-way, from quasi-Black control of Black schools to practically total white control. (p. 118)

I support my argument by first reviewing Vanessa Siddle Walker's (2000) study of segregated black high schools from 1935 to 1965. Walker's work is important because it revises the erroneous notion that black schools and black educators were uniformly inferior to white schools and educators. Walker's work provides knowledge of what filled the void about which Haynes spoke. After reviewing Walker's work, I then provide support from my own analysis of the Black Educators Association's history books. My focus here is on the struggle waged at both the national and state levels to incorporate black history into the curriculum and protect African American children from the racist content of textbooks. I then discuss desegregation and its effect on the employment status of African American educators. My aim is to demonstrate the extent of the power vacuum created by the systematic elimination of black principals. I conclude by discussing the implications of faculty desegregation policies with regard to hidden curriculum and white educators controlling predominately black schools.

"VALUED SEGREGATED SCHOOLS"

Vanessa Siddle Walker's (2000) recent review of research regarding segregated black schools from 1935 to 1965 demonstrates that segregated black schools, though shamefully underfunded, were nevertheless valuable to and valued by the black community. Walker begins by noting that research has traditionally focused only on quantifiable inequities between black schools in comparison to white schools. She explains that this traditional focus has resulted in an incomplete and inaccurate portrait of black schools as compared to white schools and argues this is due in part to researchers' reliance on archival material and the fact that these same researchers were unfamiliar with black schools aside from survey data and cursory visits. In short, the quality of education was never an issue. With regard to this old line of research, Walker (2000) notes that African American schools are "depicted as inferior because of inequality in facilities, lack of transportation, shorter school terms, teacher-pupil conflicts, overcrowding, poor teacher and poor student attendance . . . quantitative differences in I.Q. levels between Black and White students, library books, school lunch availability, and other easily measured variables" (p. 253). Additionally, African American parents and students are "portrayed as complacent or appreciative recipients of the contributions of philanthropic organizations" (p. 253).

Walker explains that research focus shifted during the last two decades as researchers began to focus on the quality of education provided by African American educators prior to desegregation. She notes that, more recently, research has utilized oral interview and ethnography as methods of inquiry. Her findings concede the presence of inequality but also reveal that the pedagogical tradition practiced in black schools were, as was noted above, valuable to the community and valued by the community. Earlier research failed to reveal the good things about the schools, including the caring behavior of teachers and students, support of parents, institutional support for students, and the high expectations the school and community placed on the black children. Walker (2000) notes that because this more recent research is not well known "scholars continue to reference the schools with an understanding of the earlier research that captures inequalities, but with little recognition of the subsequent studies that expand the historical picture" (p. 255). My contention is that this incomplete and inaccurate portrait is damaging in the sense that it contributes to the present negative image of black educators by failing to highlight the important historical roles they performed by providing valued educational services despite enormously difficult circumstances.

Walker's aim is to address this problem by providing a synthesis of the more recent studies and "delineating what is known—and what is not known—about the segregated African American schools in the south" (p. 255). Her article provides a review of the studies that focused on black schools from 1935 to 1969, a period that corresponded with the emergence of widespread state-supported education for African Americans and concluded with the dismantling of dual school systems. Walker's data consists of seventeen studies that use case histories, surveys, and interviews of people who attended or taught in particular schools. She summarizes her findings and implications as follows:

> A most significant finding of this review is that none of this scholarship contradicts the earlier historical accounts in their frank description of inequality. To the contrary, they confirm the presence and injustice of a system that failed to meet the needs of some of its students based on color. However, the studies do extend understanding of the schools by providing an up-close view of the education that occurred in these settings and they stand in opposition to the studies that depict African American segregated schooling as unilaterally inferior. What emerges in these accounts is a particular kind of schooling born of the struggles associated with inequality, but nevertheless associated with successful schooling practices in the minds of constituents and on some limited objective criteria. The consistency of this perspective demands that it be welded into a comprehensive understanding of the era of segregated education. (Walker, 2000, p. 277)

Walker (2000) argues that four themes can be drawn from the various studies: curriculum and extracurricular activities, leadership of the school principal, and exemplary teachers. In the following paragraphs, I review her findings with respect to the first three.

Concerning the curriculum and extracurricular traditions, African American educators and communities alike insisted that black children be taught the same academic curriculum available at white schools. At the time, the New England Classical liberal curriculum was that model. In some cases, efforts were made to even exceed the academic courses offered at white schools; however, these efforts were often derailed by school boards intent on maintaining an advantage for white students. Moreover, according to Walker, black educators found it necessary to blend the New England model in a way that gave African American children a special form of education consistent with their commitment to racial uplift. Walker explains that black students took both classical and vocational courses; hence, African American schools resembled white schools to the extent that unequal funding allowed and that African American educators could innovate. In addition to the formal curriculum, and when finances allowed, students participated in extracurricular activities (e.g., glee club, rhythm band, choral club, band, dance orchestra, newspaper, Beta club, library club) and athletics. Students also participated in special observances such as Negro History Week and Emancipation Proclamation Day, which were formalized in a sense but not written into the official curriculum.

Concerning the leadership role of the principal, Walker explains that he was "the single central figure in the segregated school" (p. 272). Due to his position and to the fact that he was the most highly educated person in the community, he had many roles—including "chief fundraiser" for the school, "leader of local initiatives to help the African American community," "chief instructional leader" of the school, "marriage counselor, and financial advisor, role model," and "middle man" between the black community and the white power structure. She cites Rogers's 1967 study that describes the principal as "a superintendent, supervisor, family counselor, financial advisor, community leader, and employer":

> The man who headed this important community structure, the principal was the man who ran the school and, in many cases, the black community. His influence in community affairs was almost without exception great. He was, therefore, central in community life and was indeed more knowledgeable about what was going on than anyone else. Also, as head of the Black high school, he had a role in the White power structure as well. This usually put him in the position of knowing more about the larger community than any other Black in the Black Community . . . When we say that the high school played a major role in the functioning of the community and in its development, this implies that the principal of the Black high school played a major role in the functioning and development of this community because of the importance of his role in the school. (Walker, 2000, p. 276)

Concerning exemplary teachers, Walker explains that they "appear to have worked with the assumption that their job was to be certain that children learned the material presented" (p. 265). In addition, she noted the consistency of language used to describe teachers: they held "high expectations," were "demanding," "made sure you got your lesson," "would not let you fail," and made students "stay after school as long as necessary to learn" (Walker, 2000, p. 276). Teachers were also said to have taken on enormous amounts of extra responsibility, including holding extracurricular tutoring sessions, visiting student's homes and churches, purchasing school supplies for their classrooms, and clothing and college scholarship aid for children from families without financial means. Moreover, by the 1950s African American teacher preparation exceeded that of white teachers in many southern states. Walker notes that in a few schools, several teachers held PhDs and many also participated in continuing professional training by attending summer school and traveling to state and even national conventions. Walker found that many of the schools boasted of 100 percent membership in teachers associations that provided journals and newsletters, which kept them abreast of national trends in education. She concludes, "African American teachers were professional educators steeped in an understanding of philosophies about children and teaching as well as their own set of beliefs about how the children should be motivated to achieve" (p. 266).

BLACK EDUCATORS' ASSOCIATIONS AND THE STRUGGLE FOR BLACK HISTORY

Walker points out that both the old and new line of research focuses primarily on individual schools; very little focus has been placed on the organizational structure of black educators at the local, state, and national level (Walker, 2000). My analysis of black educators' associations' history results in several themes, of which I will discuss only one. The struggle to institute Negro History Week in black schools is a core theme in many books. This demonstrates that having black control of schools provided the opportunity to deflect racist curriculum material aimed at black children. For instance, the establishment of Black History Week coincided with the establishment of the committee on social science, which was commissioned by the federal government in 1912. The creation of this committee led to the establishment of the Hampton Social Studies model as the national social studies curriculum with the

1916 publication of its final report, *Social Studies in Secondary Education*. This is important because the Hampton Social Studies model was a racist curriculum model designed with the aim of socializing blacks to accept a subservient position in American society. Also in 1912, Carter G. Woodson established Associated Publishers with the aim being to "make possible the publication and circulation of valuable books on the Negro not acceptable to most publishers" (Perry, 1975, p. 193). This could be interpreted to mean that the establishment of Associated Publishers was a reaction of black educators to the government's educational agenda for blacks.

A careful analysis leads one to conclude that the implementation of black history into the curriculum was part of the agenda of many, if not all, black state teachers associations. In 1925, the American Teachers Association's (ATA) findings committee recommended "an increased study of Negro History in our schools." Perry includes a very important discussion regarding the establishment of Negro history week in black schools, crediting Carter G. Woodson with undertaking

> the Herculean effort to accelerate the writing of this subject matter; [providing] vehicles for publishing and systematizing the whole area of study; [stimulating] scholars to rewrite history by means of scholarly research and scientific methodology. It was his role to spread Negro history throughout the schools and colleges of the U.S., especially the black schools; to provide scholarships and grants for young blacks to study history; to establish a repository for historical documents and writings, keeping them available for research purposes of students and scholars, and preserving them for posterity; and to develop overall a sense of racial identity and pride in black people. It was the most ambitious program that had ever been conceived with regard to Negro history, and Woodson actually developed it. (Perry, 1975, p. 193)

Perry explains that Woodson's goal was to reach black children directly and through their teachers.

In its merger agreement with the National Education Association (NEA), the ATA made explicit its commitment to the study of black history by demanding the continued relationship between the ATA and the Association of the Study of Afro-American Life and History in the promotion of African American History Week. In addition, the NEA established the Carter G. Woodson Award, which was to be presented yearly to an NEA affiliate or to a nominee chosen by an NEA affiliate for leadership in promoting African American History Week. The agreement also required the NEA to commemorate Black History Week every year by sponsoring an observance at its headquarters and distributing materials to affiliates. The NEA also agreed to encourage local and state associations to help secure proclamations from governors and mayors.

Woodson's influence can be seen in the ambitions and work of various state teachers associations. During a 1925 convention in Durham, the North Carolina association proclaimed in a report, "We earnestly recommend the increased study of Negro history in our schools" (Murray, 1984). The North Carolina association also initiated and published a project on Africa's contribution to world culture.

Likewise, the South Carolina association reorganized its history department in 1935 in order to make Negro history a specific focus. In 1949, at the Florida State Teachers Association convention, the social studies department's theme of Negro contributions supplied the missing pages in teaching history, and one of the discussion sessions was titled "Integrating the Contribution of the Negro in American History Classes" (Porter and Leedell, 1977). The Virginia association is mentioned as having insisted at their yearly convention that Negro teachers and students acquaint themselves with the "Negro Year Book, with Negro makers of History, with the Negro in Literature and Art," and with the Negro History Bulletin (Porter and Leedell, 1977).

The Alabama State Teachers Association's (ASTA) book dedicated the most space describing its efforts to implement black history through its Negro History Project. The book explains that the core of the project was research on African American life and history and its various studies were included in the yearbooks published by ASTA in 1931. The group's 1936 yearbook stated that the goals of the project was to ensure "the presence of Negro history textbooks in all public and private schools . . . [the] formation of a course of study in black history, the development of creative expressions by Negro scholars leading to essays books, monographs, and scientific research by and about black people . . . the development of a more tolerant relationship between the races, and [to] increase awareness and pride among Negro people of their contributions to ancient and modern civilization." The project also included a source book and syllabus on Negro life and education to be used in white colleges. ASTA not only distributed Negro History Project study kits to black teachers throughout Alabama, but also made its support of black history explicit in the terms of its merger agreement. One study associated with ASTA's Negro History Project was an analysis of sixty history and civics textbooks being used by southern elementary and high schools.

The establishment of textbook committees was also a relatively frequent occurrence during the 1920s and 1930s. The Louisiana Colored Teachers Association, for example, formed a committee to review public school textbooks (Middleton, 1984). The South Carolina association also formed textbook review committees and made explicit in their merger agreement their aim "to examine and evaluate critically curriculum materials, teaching methods, pre-service and in-service education of teachers, and other sources for their proper contribution to the concepts of the worth of the individual and of appreciation of different cultural attributes" (Middleton, 1984, p. 192). Concerning textbooks, the merger agreement between the ATA and the NEA specified that "until such time as textbooks give adequate coverage to Negro history, the merged association shall celebrate the traditional Negro History Week by giving fair recognition in the February journal and other publications, and shall maintain active affiliation with the association for the study of Negro Life and History" (Middleton, 1984, p. 261).

Together, my analysis of teacher associations' histories and Walker's analysis of black schools provide the basis upon which I argue that black control of black schools was a source of power. In addition, an understanding of this history provides a historical basis for understanding the implications of faculty desegregation for African Americans.

THE DISPLACEMENT OF BLACK EDUCATORS

Contempt for black educators can be seen from the Supreme Court's initial *Brown* decision, which made no mention of black educators even after the Topeka, Kansas, board sent a form letter in 1953 to all black educators notifying them that they would be fired in the event that segregation was ruled unconstitutional. Also, in the 1956 Moberly, Missouri, case, the Supreme Court ruled that the local education board had the right to fire black teachers regardless of tenure or certification (Tillman, 2004). This decision actually gave power to control the implementation of desegregation to local boards—who were segregationists. Moreover, in the 1992 *Freeman v. Pitts* case concerning the unitary status of the Dekalb County school system in suburban Atlanta, the district court ruled against unitary status on the grounds that the system had only achieved unitary status in four areas: student assignment, transportation, facilities, and extracurricular activities. The appellate court ruled against the district court on the grounds that improvement had to be made in the other two areas, teacher and principal assignments. The Supreme Court then overruled the appellate ruling, stating that unitary status can be achieved on a piecemeal basis (Bankston and Caldas, 2002, p. 44).

The contempt for black educators also reveals itself in the *Guidelines for Desegregation of Schools*, issued in 1964 by the Department of Housing, Education and Welfare (HEW) and commissioned by the Office of Civil Rights. The guidelines contained no language concerning the hiring, dismissal, or promotion of black educators. In addition, an NEA official quoted a HEW attorney concerning the absence of language about black educators as saying, "In a war there must be some casualties and perhaps the black teacher will be the causalities in the fight for equal education of black students" (Tillman, 2004, p. 287). This inaction on behalf of the Office of Civil Rights and HEW effectively left power to control the desegregation of educators in the hands of all-white local education boards.

According to Linda Tillman (2004), approximately 39,000 African American principals were displaced as a consequence of faculty desegregation policies, including 90 percent of all African American high school principals. With Walker's description of the principal's importance in mind, this represented a tremendous loss of black control over the education of black children and opened a tremendous power vacuum. Several other studies have addressed the issue of disappearing black principals. One, published by the National Center for Research and Information on Equal Education Opportunity (NCRIEEO), reveals desegregation's devastating blow to black principals:

In Texas 600 Black Principals were lost between 1964 and 1970.
In Delaware 44 Black Principals were lost between 1964 and 1970.
In W. Virginia 200 Black principals were lost between 1964 and 1970.
(Adair 1984, p. 15)

A study carried out by a Senate subcommittee on education reports the following numbers:

- In Alabama between 1966 and 1970 the number of black high school principals dropped from 210 to 57, and black junior high principals dropped from 141 to 54.
- In Arkansas between 1963 and 1971 the number of black high school principals dropped from 134 to 14.
- In Florida between 1965 and 1970 the number of black high school principals dropped from 102 to 13.
- In Georgia between 1968 and 1970, 66 black principals were eliminated while 75 white principals added.
- In Kentucky between 1965 and 1969, the number of black principals dropped from 350 to 36 (of these 36, 22 were in Louisville).
- In Louisiana between 1968 and 1970, 68 black principals were eliminated and 68 white principals added.
- In Mississippi over 250 black administrators were displaced in a 2-year period.
- In Maryland there were 44 black high school principals in 1954 and 31 in 1968, whereas there were 167 white high school principals in 1954 and 280 in 1968.
- In North Carolina between 1963 and 1970, the number of black high school principals dropped from 227 to 8.
- In South Carolina between 1965 and 1970, the number of black high school principals dropped from 114 to 13.
- In Tennessee the number of black high school principals dropped from 73 to 17.
- In Virginia between 1965 and 1970, the number of black high school principals dropped from 170 to 6.

The subcommittee report goes on to present more extensive numbers on the impact on individual counties in Alabama:

- In 1966–1967 there was at least 1 black principal in each of the 67 systems; in 1970–1971 there were 30 counties with no black principals.
- In 1966–1967 there were only 6 county systems with no black senior high principals; in 1970–1971 there were 17.
- In 1966–1967 there were 25 county systems with no black junior high principals; in 1970–1971 there were 42.
- In 1966–1967 there were no black elementary principals in 17 systems; in 1970–1971 there were 38.
- In 1966–1967 there were 6 city systems that had no black principals; in 1970–1971 there were 25.
- In 1966–1967 there were 12 city systems that had no black senior high principals; in 1970–1971 there were 42.
- In 1966–1967 there were 41 city systems with no black junior high principals; in 1970–1971 there were 46.
- In 1966–1967 there were no black elementary school principals in 24 city systems; in 1970–1971 there were none in 40.

THE MERGER OF STATE EDUCATORS ASSOCIATIONS

Another consequence of desegregation was the loss of black teachers associations. In 1954, there were dual state officials in 18 states. The impetus for the dual state associations to merge was the 1964 Civil Rights Act. The day after President Lyndon Johnson's pronouncement, the NEA issued Resolution 12, which ordered affiliates to remove all language concerning race from their constitutions and make plans to merge before January 1, 1966. The dual associations in 7 states had merged by 1965; however, the 11 states of the Deep South maintained dual associations. In 1966 and 1967, Florida, South Carolina, Tennessee, Texas, and Virginia formed unitary associations in compliance with the NEA's merger mandate. According to many black educators, the problem with the merger agreements was that they failed to assure black representation in leadership positions (Middleton, 1984). According to Perry (1975), the NEA enlisted the help of administrators who applied pressure on black principals and teachers to accept merger agreements. She argues that they had little choice.

Moreover, the NEA's president acknowledged concerns of black educators regarding the shortcomings of the merger agreements between the first waves of association mergers, and as a result, the executive committee required the creation of "entirely new" associations with guaranteed minority representation on key committees and staff for six years and two-thirds vote on major issues (Middleton, 1984). In addition, a new deadline of January 1, 1969, was established for the submission of merger plans. Alabama, Arkansas, and Georgia met the deadline, but white affiliates in Louisiana and Mississippi and the black affiliates in North Carolina continued to hold out. The North Carolina Teachers Association eventually accepted the plan and Mississippi soon followed. The Louisiana affiliates were the last holdouts; the LEA and LTA maintained separate teachers associations until they merged in 1977.

Concerning the merger agreements, former LEA president Volver Williams is quoted as saying:

> After we had complied with every aspect of membership in NEA in a loyal and faithful way, then without any reason we found ourselves defending ourselves, justifying ourselves, as being its affiliate in this state. Whereas the LTA had voted unanimously to get out of the NEA because of what they said were NEA liberal views on integration, desegregation and that kind of thing . . . We saw what happened in all of the other southern states that had acquiesced to the NEA mandate for merger. In my opinion, black educators no longer existed in any viable and visible leadership role in those merged associations. In almost every instance the executive secretaries were white people, the leaders were white people. Those merger agreements spelled out alternate years for black leadership and white leadership, but with only five or six years' worth of guarantees—after that you were on your own. I don't think the NEA was a friend of black people. I don't think it is now. (Middleton, 1984, p. 132)

Like each of the other NEA-affiliated black state associations, the LEA was forced into a "merger" agreement that assured it of six years of representation at the leadership level. The consolidation plan, like that of the other "merger" plans between black educators associations and their white counterparts in the South, spelled out its doom. The consequence of the merger was that the African American community lost an organization that had represented its educational and political interests for three-quarters of a century (Middleton, 1984).

CURRICULUM IMPLICATIONS: THE HIDDEN CURRICULUM

The racial structure of a school's faculty is part of the school curriculum. Apple (2004) explains, "Schools, therefore, 'process' both knowledge and people. In essence, the formal and informal knowledge is used as a complex filter to process people, often by class; and, at the same time, different dispositions and values are taught to different school populations, again often by class (sex and race)" (p. 32). The covert form of knowledge is what reproduction theorists refer to as the *hidden curriculum*. Apple defines the hidden curriculum as "the norms and values that are implicitly, but effectively, taught in schools and that are not usually talked about in teachers' statements of ends or goals" (pp. 78–79). A predominately white faculty structure reinforces notions of white supremacy and thereby assists in reproducing the status quo.

According to a 1998 study regarding the employment of black teachers, black students made up 16.2 percent of the nation's public school population, whereas black teachers accounted for only 8.2 percent of all teachers. Moreover, 73 percent of school teachers in inner-city schools were white while in many inner-city areas black students made up over 80 percent of the school population. The article explains that this is part of the reason that black children do poorly in schools: "A major reason why black students don't do as well in school is that too many black kids are being taught by white teachers—teachers who do not provide role models and who think badly about the abilities of black kids from the moment they enter the classroom ("JBHE Ranks the States," 1998, p. 25).

Gary Howard (2006) argues that it is necessary to raise the cultural competence of white teachers, particularly as it relates to race. He argues, "I am convinced there is a prior and equally compelling need for White people, particularly White educators in the United States and other nations of the West, to look within ourselves and realign our deepest assumptions and perceptions regarding the racial marker that we carry, namely Whiteness" (p. 6). Drawing from over 40 years of addressing multicultural education and numerous encounters with educators, he cogently argues that white teachers "need to understand the dynamics of the past and present dominance, face how we [white educators] have been shaped by myths of superiority, and begin to sort out our thoughts, emotions, and behaviors relative to race and other dimension of diversity" (p. 6). He explains that when white teachers profess to be colorblind, they are unaware of the historical institutional practices that systemically favor certain racial groups. Howard concludes by noting that an unexamined reflection of the nature of white dominance limits the approach to corrective action that could lead to social justice. The reluctance or inability of white teachers to see or acknowledge racism has consequences regarding the education of students of color. Apple (2004) explains that the role that conflict has played in social progress is not a part of the official history. Apple notes that black studies and women's studies counter this aspect of the curriculum: "Here, struggle and conflict on a communal basis is often explicitly and positively focused upon" (p. 90). This point illuminates the value of black educators and need for black educators to design and implement curriculum relevant to African Americans' positions in capitalist social relations. Furthermore, all things being equal, black teachers are more likely to be critical of unjust societal structures. Apple explains that successful teachers of black children must be able to engage them in reflections about the status quo. Conversely, curriculums that are based on white supremacist ideas are more effectively implemented by white teachers. This is important considering the fact that curricula have traditionally been designed for black children with the aim of making them accept racial subservience (Anderson, 1988; Watkins, 2001).

REFERENCES

Adair, A. (1984). *Desegregation: The illusion of black progress*. Lanham, MD: University Press of America.

Anderson, J. (1988). *The education of blacks in the south, 1860–1935*. Chapel Hill: University of North Carolina Press.

Apple, M. (2004). *Ideology and curriculum*. New York: Routledge.

Bankston, C. and Caldas, S. (2002). *A troubled dream: The promise and failure of school desegregation in Louisiana*. Nashville, TN: Vanderbilt University Press.

Howard, G. (2006). *We can't teach what we don't know: White teachers in multicultural schools*. New York: Teachers College Press.

JBHE ranks the states in the employment of black teachers. (1998). *Journal of Blacks in Higher Education 21,* 25–27.

Middleton, E. (1984). *History of the Louisiana education association*. Washington, DC: National Education Association.

Murray, P. (1984). *History of the North Carolina teachers association*. Washington, DC: National Education Association.

Perry, T (1975). *History of the American teachers association*. Washington, DC: National Education Association.

Porter, G., and Leedell, W. (1977). *The history of the Florida state teachers association*. Washington, DC: National Education Association.

Tillman, L. (2004). (Un)Intended consequences? The impact of the Brown v. Board of Education decision on the employment status of black educators. *Education and Urban Society 36*(3), 280–303.

Veteran Educator Bemoans Loss of Negro Teachers and Principals. (1968, October 6). *The Baton Rouge Advocate*.

Walker, V. (2000). Valued segregated school for African American children in the South, 1935–1969: A review of common themes and characteristics. *Review of Educational Research, 70*(3), 253–85.

Watkins, W. (2001). *The white architects of black education: Ideology and power in America, 1865–1954*. New York: Teachers College Press.

CHAPTER 2

The Context of African American Educational Performance

Na'im Akbar

There has been a persisting and ongoing debate and discussion regarding the educational performance of urban (meaning African American and Latino) youth. From the George W. Bush administration's educational initiative named No Child Left Behind to a plethora of local-, state-, and even community-initiated programs, efforts abound in the attempt to identify the source and eliminate the significant disparities in "minority" academic achievement. The methods for identifying the nature of these disparities, as well as speculations about their origins, have been superficial at best and grossly inadequate at worst, leading to very little improvement in the educational problems faced by African Americans in public education systems.

For the most part, the issue of educational performance has been reduced to an issue of "evaluation," based on the dependency of various dubious tools of alleged mental measurement. Dr. R. Grann Lloyd, former editor of the *Negro Educational Review*, in a volume reissued some years ago in a book edited by Dr. Asa Hilliard titled *Testing African American Students* (1991), observed:

> The confusion about the central purpose of education and the basic function of America's public schools . . . seems to have spawned and fostered the notion that the salvation of our nation and our schools requires that we concentrate on testing school children rather than on teaching them; on blaming and embarrassing school children for low test scores instead of teaching and nourishing them; decapitating prospective teachers professionally by holding them up to public ridicule and scorn, before they can even begin their teaching careers,

because of their test scores rather than encouraging them and teaching them how to teach children. (p. 35)

Dr. Lloyd's comments, which were meaningful in the early 1990s when they were penned, were almost prophetic in predicting the expansion of educational policy that continues to build on the faulty assumptions that the solution to the educational problem rests in the expansion of evaluation, assessment, and testing. In the early days of the first administration of President George W. Bush, the dubious use of testing reached the level of national policy as the hallmark of an educational policy intended to ensure that "no child would be left behind" educationally. This policy was not based on any process of systemic educational change, but was instead focused on identifying and assessing evidence of disparities in educational achievement. Diagnosis has grown to be sufficient without any strategies for intervention, except to expand the diagnostic process.

As is typical in Western scientific thought, information that is most highly valued is reduced to some form of quantification and the numbers are labeled as if the number and label were sufficient intervention to change the implications of the numbers. In other words, test scores and educational performance have been made synonymous and the assumption is that the improvement of test scores (of dubious validity) is a measure of improvement in the educational process.

HISTORICAL CONTEXT OF BLACK EDUCATION

The major assumption that guides European American educational systems is the idea that the educational process entails the demonstrated internalization of a selected body of information. Well-educated or high-performing students are assumed to be capable of mastering significantly more of that body of information than the low-performing or less well-educated group. Those who demonstrate less ability to internalize this body of information are considered to be inferior to those who do manifest high internalization, and the lesser are ultimately suspected of having limited endowment with mental ability. The logical leap from poor school performance to evaluations for special education to the ultimate conclusion of deficient mental capacity is a common pattern that emerges. There have been recurring cycles in the evaluation of learning abilities when the conclusion that the disparate school performance and relatively disparate performance of black students was indicative of inferior intelligence as a consequence of race.

Public school education is a system. It entails curricular content, social interactions, policy, economics, and a context of social and cultural arrangements and assumptions. Education is not a sterile, isolated body of information that is infused into the passive and receptive brains of young students. Education is a dynamic and multifaceted system that occurs within the broad context of all of the variables noted above. That means that the educational system is not a simple input-output arrangement as is implied by the evaluation model described above where input is measured by sampling amounts of the pool of information that has been internalized.

In this discussion, I want to suggest that education must be understood within the broader context that surrounds the instructional process. In the specific instance of understanding the education of African American children, there are some very important historical variables that must be considered in order to understand the problems posed by the educational system in its current form. One of the conclusions that have been reached from the Western concept of education and evaluation is that the reason for the relatively poor performance of African American students is that these young people for a variety of social, cognitive, economic, and even genetic reasons are somehow ill suited for formal education. The conclusion has been reached repeatedly that there is some deficiency in these children and seldom if ever has the question been raised of the possible deficiencies of the educational system.

It is important to recognize that African American children in the twenty-first century represent the continuation of a historical process that has been in place since the 1619 entrance of the earliest Africans brought as captives to America. Though this nearly four-centuries-old date sounds too remote to be relevant, it sets a very unique and brutally relevant context for understanding twenty-first-century education in America. The first factor that is mandated by the designation of this historical context is the incomparability of the African American educational experience. No other racial or national group in America began their educational experience under the conditions of America's system of chattel slavery. For the first two-and-a-half centuries of African presence in America, education was not only unavailable, but even more significantly, it was prohibited. The prohibition was not simply in regard to attendance at educational centers, but also any evidence of Africans acquiring information that would equip them with literacy or computational skills was a crime punishable by brutal executions of justice such as beatings or mutilations. In other words, "book learning" was not permissible for the Africans (slaves). Only those skills that furthered the objectives and economic well-being of the plantation owner and his objectives were taught to the captured Africans.

Reading skills and possession of books became contraband for slaves and there were few infractions more serious, especially in the Deep South, than slaves teaching each other how to read. Even compassionate whites who were found to teach Africans some rudimentary skills of literacy were viewed as serious violators of the social (and in some instances the legal) code. Frederick Douglas (1845), in his autobiography *My Bondage and My Freedom*, observes:

> When I went back to the Eastern Shore, and was at the house of Master Thomas, I was neither allowed to teach, nor to be taught. The whole community—with but a small exception, among the Whites—frowned on everything like imparting instruction either to slaves or to free colored persons . . . At our second meeting, I learned there was some objection to the existence of the Sabbath school; and sure enough, we had scarcely got at work—*good work*, simply teaching a few colored children how to read the gospel of the Son of God—when in rushed a mob, headed by Mr. Wright Fairbanks and Mr. Garrison West—two class leaders and Master Thomas; who armed with sticks and other missiles, drove us off, and commanded us never to meet for such a purpose again. (pp. 155–156)

Needless to say, the earliest African experience with American education was its strict prohibition. Many of the Africans captured and brought to America were from highly literate and academically advanced African societies such as the country of Mali, the home of the Ancient University of Jenne' and Timbuktu. Despite the prohibitions against learning, many of these Africans maintained a memory and strong desire to cultivate the skills they had been introduced to in their native lands. In addition, the idea that education was contraband and viewed as a potential leveler in the social "disorder" that had placed the Africans at the oppressive feet of whites who so jealously protected their rights to literacy made the access to education even more appealing. In spite of this aspiration to learn, most of the first three centuries that Africans spent in captivity in America was in a context where education was clearly prohibited to the African. Just the acquisition of literacy alone was a punishable offense.

PHASE II OF BLACK EDUCATION IN AMERICA

With the legal emancipation of the slaves in 1865, there was the gradual appearance of the next evolution of educational experience for Africans in America. Somewhat surprising was the widespread presence of Africans who had obtained literacy through the underground system and had acquired this "illegal" learning. Small schools and study groups sprang up in nearly every setting where there were newly freed people from enslavement. Despite the limited education they had, they quickly began to spread the limited reading, writing, and computational skills among themselves, especially to their young people. It was recognized that education was a key tool for freedom. Education was highly valued by the Africans. From the rapid spread of schools established by missionaries and Reconstructionists that quickly filled with students, the former captives were highly motivated to learn. When one reflects on the large number of colleges that were started before the end of the nineteenth century—only 35 years after the Emancipation Proclamation—it was evident that education of blacks was a growth industry that was enthusiastically pursued by the newly freed population.

It is important to keep in mind that in spite of the fact that education moved from an underground activity to an open and highly popular activity following Emancipation, within the context of the American education system, black education was still considered to be a highly restricted activity that was the relatively exclusive arena of white (males, especially). Education, as it was available to white men, was still considered to be an exclusive territory. Either by de facto or actual legal restrictions, blacks were not permitted to be educated in the same environment as whites. In fact, for the next 90 years (1865–1955), the segregation of the races in educational settings was the law in most of the former slave states and was the practice of choice in the rest of the United States. The assumption continued to reign that (1) the learning capacity of blacks was different from that of whites and (2) blacks did not "need to know" what was taught to white males. So even in the black-run segregated schools, there was the unwritten assumption that blacks needed a "special education" that was ultimately considered to be inferior to white education. The famous debate between W. E. B. Du Bois and Booker T. Washington centered around this question of the nature of black education—whether it should be exclusively vocational (opined Washington) or grooming of the "talented tenth" for leadership of the race (opined Du Bois). In any event, it was a priority that blacks should remain outside of white educational settings regardless of the content of their education. Of course, there were isolated cases of small cadres of blacks receiving education in traditionally white educational settings, such as Oberlin College in Ohio, a major stop on the Underground Railroad. Almost from the time of Emancipation, blacks in small and isolated numbers began to matriculate at major white universities. Even W. E. B. Du Bois himself graduated from Harvard in 1890. Despite his exemplary performance and graduating cum laude in his class, he reports a very segregated social life and environment while at Harvard (1968, pp. 135–38).

The educational system in general and particularly the curriculum was a key element to the maintenance of a white supremacist society and power structure in the United States. Segregation kept the educational system free of internal critique or question. It was an environment for the exaltation of white European-American culture and intellect and an environment for the systematic degradation or exclusion of African culture and intellect. The educational system was constructed to insure the preservation of the power, authority, and hegemony of white (male) culture. Since this system of education benefited the exclusive consumers, then there was no real incentive to critique the system for its exclusionary policies.

THE CONTEMPORARY EDUCATIONAL CONTEXT

The contemporary alienation of African American youth from the educational system is an accurate reading of the historical and continuous basic form of American education as intentionally, defiantly, and persistently a "white educational system." Even with the kind of self-destructive rebellion that characterizes the response of black youth, it is important to give credibility to the validity of their analysis. This is not to excuse the self-destructive conduct of black youth who have failed to find an adaptive resolution for this conflict. Neither does it forgive the responsibility of African American communities to rise up in the wake of such educational opposition and do as we did on the plantations and post-plantation in America and that is to make opportunities, even when they are not given. This means that we must apply the same defiance and determination that marshaled us through the restrictions of segregated educational systems and turned the restrictive liability into an asset, providing the leadership and vision that opened new horizons for us and for America. In other words, the resistance of the system does not demand failure. Failure is not a failing score on some national achievement test; failure is to permit a generation of young people to lose access to opportunity because of a passive acceptance of their failure in an educational system that has always required us to overcome the odds and find a strategy of perseverance.

Though changes have continued to occur in the educational system, since slavery and since the nearly one hundred years of post-slavery segregation, surprisingly much of the structure, context, and content of the educational system has remained unchanged. Of course, the quantification of the disparate performance of African American youth fails to take account of this overwhelming but shadowed reality of the American educational system. In reality, what is being defined as education fails to provide for the intellectual and personal needs of non-white children. It does not motivate or inform, nor does it inspire people who are systematically excluded from the educational content and the context of information mastery. The seldom discussed fact is that despite the evidence that there is a disproportionate number of under-performing African American children, the majority of these children are ignored and alienated by an educational system that discounts their existence and their reality actually manage to succeed in this system. It would be interesting to note what would be the case if the tables were turned and white children were being educated in a system that ignored them in its curriculum and its educational values. If there was some compelling reason to compare the performance of white and African American children, the only valid comparison would be to evaluate the performance of white children in a similarly alien educational environment as is the educational environment of African American children who are expected to master European American hegemony, its values and information that informs a system of white supremacy.

The unfortunate consequence of the mastery by these comparable and even higher-achieving African American children is a sacrifice of their personal dignity and self-respect. Though, according to the tests, these African American youth have achieved well, they have taken in toxic information about themselves. Without proper guidance and support to help them screen information, they have inadvertently internalized a body of knowledge that can have morbid consequences on their self-esteem. The most effective adjustment is to successfully develop what Du Bois (1903/1989) called a "double consciousness." With this kind of adaptive schizoid adjustment they become "white" in the educational world and struggle to maintain a positive cultural identity in their own world. Without the sense of their double identity they become minimally capable of advancing the collective good of their own communities because their alien education (called "mis-education" by Dr. Carter G. Woodson [1933]) has failed to equip them with the skills to know themselves and to advance their collective good.

The African American so-called failures in the educational system are unable to negotiate the painful personality split and reject the educational system including its valuable assets of social mobility, economic solvency, political empowerment, and general social acceptance by the people who are represented in the educational system. Even in their rejection of the educational system, they join their "successful" peers in the internalization of the implicit values of the shadow curriculum of American education that continues to imply that literacy, educational competence, and even academic success is the reserved and special privilege of whites and nonwhites who flaunt their mastery of white supremacy values. In a very self-destructive way, they equate intellectual prowess with white identity. They experience these successes of the educational system with animosity and alienation. The hip-hop culture reflects these attitudes in their contemptuous commentary on education, Standard English, and conventional values. Even though the commentary has historical and political validity, it fails to provide effective navigation around the barriers to success that are constructed with the bricks of alienation from the educational system and mainstream European American culture. Unfortunately, African American students who innocently manage to succeed in the educational system and are privileged to wear the symbolic crown of alien educational achievement are forced to endure the ostracism of their peers who have rejected the destructive education system that requires them to adopt an alien identity in order to succeed. So these young students are faced with the paradox of success in the Euro-centered educational system of America, which means failure within one's community and in oneself. With the certainty of the dual identity (black and American) they are required to critique the errors of their "mis-education," apply useful educational skills to the advancement of their communities, and keep intact the vital self-esteem that permits them to be of service to themselves and humanity as a whole.

The irony is that the struggle for equal educational opportunity required African Americans to struggle in order to join a system that would only accept them on its own terms and would actually require the denunciation of their own worth and value and complicity in pushing a white supremacy agenda. In other words, African Americans were permitted to participate in a system that by its very nature rejected them. Even with the multifaceted and extensive programs that have proclaimed efforts of multiculturalism and some diversification of the educational system, this has essentially been translated to mean—following the axiological orientation of the Western world—that there has been a quantitative change in the presence of other cultural or racial groups. When the numbers of black bodies in an educational setting increase, there are self-congratulatory claims of success, even though the curriculum and values that were established in the chartering of these institutions have remained unchanged. There are islands of cultural deference in the educational system with occasional celebrations of Black

History Month, Dr. King's birthday holiday, Cinco de Mayo, Hispanic Heritage Month, and so on, but with no fundamental restructuring of the curriculum and the learning experiences of students. It remains a fact today as it did two hundred years ago that only white, male, Judeo-Christian heterosexuals of European descent are the only group of students who can complete their studies through the Ph.D. degree and never have to consider the perspective of any other person's view of the world except their own. Every other group of students must be exposed to the worldview of some other designated group beyond themselves. In fact, the degree to which they deviate from the normative prototype (e.g., white, male, Judeo-Christian) the greater the likelihood that most of their education will be from another cultural worldview.

CONCLUSION

The approach to education in America has served a particular purpose in perpetuating a set of values and preserving a certain social arrangement since its inception. One of the techniques for preserving the arrangement that the educational system sets is the emphasis on evaluation rather than innovation in correcting failures in this system. With the emphasis on evaluation, the focus is maintained on output rather than a review of the system and assumptions of education. This serves a twofold purpose: on the one hand it protects the system that has a set of shadow objectives that are intended to preserve a certain power arrangement in society. Prior to the abolition of slavery, this shadow objective was transparent and explicit that only the powerful (white males) should have access to education, and those who were the powerless (enslaved Africans) through the prohibition of their involvement in education were doomed to remain powerless. The second purpose served by the evaluation emphasis is that those who fail to internalize the objectives of the educational system can be identified as the source of the problem and both eliminated from the educational process and from the critique of the educational system. The system preserves its integrity by continuing to serve those for whom it was established to empower and eliminates any real contenders for power by designating them as incapable of effective matriculation in the educational process. Those who remain in the system do so only at the peril of their self-dignity and the ultimate self-interest of the powerless group from which they have come. When the evaluation process eliminates the so-called failures from the system, the evaluators can claim ever-continuing success since the contradictions to the success of the system are eliminated from the system with those left behind serving as empirical evidence for the success of the educational system. In other words, "no child is left behind" within the system of education because of the process of elimination. The real process of education remains uncontested and ultimately unchanged because it continues to do what it is intended to do.

The alternative approach to reviewing the educational system that is proposed in this discussion suggests that there are flaws in the fundamental assumptions of American education, particularly as it relates to differences in cultural styles and social outcomes. The implication is that in order to effectively change education so it is more inclusive of an ever more diverse student population, one must look beyond the limited perspective of evaluating quantified outcomes. Educational systems and the process of pedagogy must be reevaluated and the substance of education must be rethought to be inclusive of a wider range of content and learning styles. The content, teaching techniques, and assumptions about knowledge that were made to preserve a social hierarchy where slavery was intended to be a permanent status, and mobility was only an exchange of power among the few, must be looked at in the light of new declarations of a more inclusive and truly democratic society. A curriculum that only teaches the accomplishments of European people because it fosters the self-esteem, motivation, and inspiration of people of European descent must be challenged because it fails to acknowledge the multicultural influences that has brought prominence to human civilization. This includes the ancient contributions of America's former slaves and the ancient cultures of the native inhabitants of the Americas against whom genocide was employed in order to develop their lands.

Ancient Africans laid out guidelines for an epistemology (way of knowing) that was based on the idea that the highest form of knowing was esoteric or knowing through the inner self. Despite the overt claim that exoteric or empirical knowledge of the outer reality is the preferred approach to knowledge, the "shadow" epistemology of Western education is deeply rooted in the idea that self-knowledge is the path to empowerment. The selective curriculum that furthers the inner exploration of the European experience (even in an approach that emphasizes the infusion of external objective information) still uses as its context and frame of reference the male Caucasian of European descent. The universal human experience is analyzed through the lens of the European American experience. Their unique experiences historically, culturally, and scientifically is the context and the criterion for determining the worth and validity of all of humanity's experiences. People are characterized as primitive, savage, heathen, backwards, advanced, civilized, and so forth by the yardstick of the European American experience. The models of intellectual and educational excellence are the Caucasian, Judeo-Christian male heterosexuals of European descent.

A more inclusive approach to learning would expand the potential of the American educational system. For example, to include Asian holistic healing that incorporates energy systems, meditation, herbs, as well as massage and surgery would greatly expand the healing potential of Western medicine beyond the allopathic approach of Greek-based medicine. An understanding of Akan and Yoruba systems of social organization and theology would help to reconcile many of the dualistic confusions of society and morality. The inclusion of broader conceptions of the world would not only resolve the haunting problem of social injustice that still plagues what is supposed to be the world's model democracy, but it also would expand the capacity of America to grow in all dimensions and not just as a material power.

This expanded approach would permit the marginalized people of this society to find a comfortable identity that validates "self" in the educational system. African Americans will be excited about becoming a master physician like Imhotep as European American boys are currently inspired to become master healers like Hippocrates. When these inner-city youth see models of themselves excelling in the laboratories as they currently see images of themselves excelling on the basketball courts, they will have the same passion about an MD as they currently have about the NBA. Young girls will be able to actualize their genius as military experts and statespersons when they are exposed to images such as the military strategist Queen Nzinga or Yaa Asantawaa, the Asante military expert and diplomat. Motivated by images of the mighty

Caesars of Rome, the kings of France and England, the Founding Fathers and statesmen of America, white males of mediocre abilities and minimal indications of real leadership skills can become president of the United States. They are inspired by these powerful images of white male leadership that actually pushes them far beyond whatever innate abilities they may have. Thus is the power of inspiration that comes from self-knowledge. When the educational system only includes a narrow selection of society's youth with the inspiration of the images of self-potential, it robs the excluded of ever having the motivation and passion to challenge existing leadership and advance humanity to its next plane of development.

This discussion argues that we can only understand the academic performance of African American youth if we have a grasp of the full historical, social, and philosophical rudiments of the educational system. It is definitely not an effort to conjure excuses for the complex nature of the problems faced by African Americans and all youth in this contemporary society. With a history of such resilience and ability to adapt, there is every reason to believe that once again African Americans will rise even from the ashes of this intellectual incineration. The current emphasis on outcome evaluation is not a sufficient analysis to determine solutions for reducing the disparity in academic achievement based on race. In order to remedy the problem, rather than simply describe it, requires an effective analysis and identification of the essential dimensions that impact the learning of children within the educational system.

REFERENCES

Douglas, F. (1845/1970). *My bondage and my freedom*. Chicago: Johnson Publishing Co.

Du Bois, W. E. B. (1903/1989). *The souls of black folk*. New York: Penguin Books.

Du Bois, W. E. B. (1968). *The autobiography of W. E. B. Du Bois*. New York: International Publishers.

Hilliard, A. G. (1991). *Testing African American children*. Morristown, NJ: Aaron Press.

Woodson, C. G. (1933). *The mis-education of the Negro*. Washington, DC: Associated Publishers.

CHAPTER 3

African American Students Achieving Academic Success

The Need for Knowledge of Self

ABUL PITRE

INTRODUCTION

With the new No Child Left Behind Act taking center stage in the twenty-first century, numerous educators have continued to be alarmed at the achievement levels of African American students in relation to white students (Comer, 1998; Delpit, 1988; Hilliard, 2004; Kunjufu, 1985). This concern has led many to look for new strategies to a seemingly unending dilemma. Several scholars have suggested and implemented new programs to help enhance the achievement level of African American students. Others have conducted research that explores ways to close the achievement gap (Murrell, 2007). Despite the positive efforts that have been made to deal with the education of African American students, large numbers of African American children still lag behind white students on standardized tests. The ineffectiveness of correcting problems such as the achievement gap, the overrepresentation of African Americans in special-education classes, and other negative variables seem to subconsciously reinforce what the architects of the "new standards" had intended from the outset: an erroneous belief that African Americans are by nature culturally inept and genetically inferior to white students.

Upon closer examination one may not clearly see the root cause of under achievement and may thereby miss the opportunity to implement a program that will be successful. It seems that in too many instances, educators are chasing the blue sky only to find that it does not exist. As educators look for ways to close the achievement gap, the proper questions have not been asked, which has resulted in educators chasing that which is not true. I use the word *untrue* to demonstrate the ineffectiveness of standards and high-stakes testing as reliable indicators of student achievement. Murrell (2007) points out, "The test score discrepancy is a symptom of a much more deeply entrenched system of privilege and educational disenfranchisement that is a major factor in academic underperformance" (p. 4). The standards and high-stakes testing frenzy that has encompassed public schools have created a *necessary illusion* that is impacting African American children. These necessary illusions have resulted in more punitive and authoritarian school policies in majority African American and Latino schools. An example of punitive school policies occurred in Louisiana where several students were severely beaten by a white school administrator (personal communication, 2005). In addition, a majority of schools focus entirely on test scores that are driven by a capitalist Euro-centered curriculum (McLaren, 2007). The result of this type of schooling has resulted in what Woodson (2008) termed *mis-education*, and it has affected thousands of African American children. The media has seized the opportunity to create a conversation regarding the achievement gap; however, the media-constructed discussion about the achievement gap has not raised the proper questions. Some of those questions include: How do we define achievement for African American students? Is our definition of achievement rooted in a Euro-centered version of achievement? Who is ultimately shaping this definition, and how might this definition benefit one group and alienate another group? Is achievement simply the passing of an exam that has no relevance to critical thinking or problem-posing education? A definition of achievement is needed to ultimately guide the process that we undertake to reach the goal of education.

DEFINING ACHIEVEMENT

Achievement as it relates to African American education should be used to evaluate student effectiveness in solving problems and creating new ideas as they relate to community building and nation building. Elijah Muhammad (1965) identifies a major aspect that educational achievement should produce among African Americans:

My people should get an education which will benefit their own people and not an education adding to the "storehouse" of their teacher. We need education, but an education which removes from us the shackles of slavery and servitude. Get an education, but not an education which leaves us in an inferior position and without a future. Get an education, but not an education that leaves us looking to the slave-master for a job. (p. 39)

Thus, achievement in this type of educational system would be different from the Euro-centered, capitalist-oriented system that serves the purpose of those who rule the society. The notion of achievement under Elijah Muhammad's program would start a process among African Americans that would help them take control of their social and educational destiny. Louis Farrakhan (1992) alludes to the importance of African Americans controlling their own education: "We don't have to ask why we should control our education. The answer is clear. We should control it because if we don't we will always be under somebody else's control" (p. 15). The educational agenda of African Americans has historically been and is even today controlled by whites in positions of power.

The education of African Americans has been largely used to control one's thinking. Carter G. Woodson illustrates eloquently how the educational system has played a major role in the mis-education of African American people. Woodson (2008) notes that:

When you control a man's thinking you do not have to worry about his actions. You do not have to tell him not to stand here or go yonder. He will find his proper place and will stay in it. You do not have to send him to the back door. He will go without being told. In fact, if there is no back door, he will cut one for his special benefit. His education makes it necessary. (p. xii)

Elijah Muhammad (1973) similarly expresses, "America's educational system has never benefited you and me, only to keep us a slave to the white man" (p. 96). Malcolm X illustrates mis-education in the following way: "Just like a dog who runs out in the woods grabs a rabbit. No matter how hungry the dog is, does he eat it? No; he takes it back and lays it at boss's feet" (Shabazz, 1970, p. 14). Malcolm X surmised that this type of dog is mis-educated. Education has performed in the past and continues today to perform the function of mis-educating too many African American students. Ultimately, educational achievement must be redefined from the perspective of African Americans. Carter G. Woodson (2008) had such in mind when he said,

> The same educational process which inspires and stimulates the oppressor with the thought that he is everything and has accomplished everything worthwhile, depresses and crushes at the same time the spark of genius in the Negro by making him feel that his race does not amount to much and never will measure up to the standards of other peoples. (p. xii)

African Americans must define educational achievement. They can no longer let those in dominant positions dictate what achievement should look like for African American students. Freire (2000) affirms, "It would be a contradiction in terms if the oppressors not only defended but actually implemented a liberating education" (p. 54). In a critical pedagogical way, Elijah Muhammad examines the duality of education that exists between the oppressed and the oppressor:

> Certainly the so-called Negroes are being schooled, but is this education the equal of that of their slave masters? No; the so-called Negroes are still begging for equal education. After blinding them to the knowledge of self and their own kind for 400 years, the slave-masters refuse to civilize the so-called Negroes into the knowledge of themselves of which they were robbed. The slave-masters also persecute and hinder anyone who tries to perform this rightful duty. (Muhammad, 1965, pp. 44–45)

In defining achievement, we must first begin with who African Americans are as a people who have been historically and contemporarily oppressed through education. A careful examination of the slave-making process reveals that this process was entirely educational. Words that have been attributed to someone named Willie Lynch symbolize the educational effort used in making a slave: "Hence, both the horse and the nigger must be broken; that is, break them from one form of mental life to another—keep the body and take the mind" (Hassan-El, 2007, p. 14). These words illustrate both the past and current dilemma in educating African American children. African American education has been controlled by those people similar to Lynch who have devised an educational plan that puts to death the creative mind of African American children. On any given day, African American students are being advised that they must keep quiet in school and pay close attention. The "good" students are those who can keep quiet and memorize answers. I call this the "keep quiet nigger child syndrome" that really says one's thinking and expressions do not really matter; what is most important is one's ability to accept the dominant group's way of thinking.

Anyon (1981), in her work on social class and the hidden curriculum of work, noted how schools reproduce what exists in the larger society. Schools that served students in the working class were involved with classroom activities that required rote memorization. These students were being prepared for working-class positions; thus, they were not engaged in critical or creative thinking. African American students are less likely to be involved in activities that stimulate critical thinking. In his book *Pedagogy of the Oppressed*, Freire (2000) gives excellent examples of how education serves the role of domesticating individuals from oppressed groups. Typically in these penal-like institutions, some African American students will become more accustomed to the banking model of education that diminishes their critical-thinking ability. As Freire (2000) notes, students in oppressive schools will not be asked to think but will be thought of as *things*. This domestication has been a primary reason for the growing dislike for school among some African American students.

KNOWLEDGE OF SELF AND CRITICAL PEDAGOGY

I would like to examine two major ideas that might help us to better understand the role of proper education in inspiring and motivating African American students. I will examine the notion of "know thyself" and critical pedagogical possibilities for enhancing the education of African American students.

As I mentioned earlier, the education of African Americans has been primarily concerned with making them better workers in a capitalist system that serves the interest of those in dominant positions. In order to reverse the mis-education that is currently taking place in school,

African American students must first be given knowledge of self. The knowledge of self will lay the base for reawakening of the black mind. Karenga (2002) notes that of all the immigrants that have come to America, the African American has been completely stripped of a true knowledge of self. Elijah Muhammad (1965) eloquently explains the *amnesia dilemma*: "Anyone who does not have a knowledge of self is considered a victim of amnesia or unconsciousness and is not very competent" (p. 39). The stripping of knowledge of self has resulted in amnesia. If asked their origin, their name, their language, or their culture, the African American is unable to reply, thus rendering them an amnesia victim. To reverse this amnesia, African Americans need a history of themselves that dates back beyond their history in America. Too often, the accomplishments of African Americans are confined to black accomplishments in white America. However, the knowledge of self is not simply about examining great African queens, kings, scientists, mathematicians, educators, and so on; it is ultimately about looking back at the relationship between the African American and God.

In his book *Know Thy Self*, Naim Akbar (1998) notes the following role of education: "The major premise of effective education must be *self-knowledge*. In order to achieve the goals of identity and empowerment that we have described above, the educational process must be one that educes the awareness of who we are" (p. 17). The process of educing this awareness is where the dilemma may lie. Akbar says, "This aspect of the education in self-knowledge creates a serious conflict for the European American educational process. The conflict is a result of the rigid separation between church and state which has been established in their concept of education" (p. 50). Another problem is that in order to educe an awareness of self, African Americans must travel back in time to uncover who they were before their arrival to America. In most schools, any discussion that will lead to a true understanding of self will create a firestorm from a wide array of people. However, to properly educate the African American student, one must consider what Akbar refers to as *transmitting acquired immunities*:

> We know now that people who have survived exposure to certain diseases are able to transmit immunity to those diseases through their genes, the mother's milk while being breast-fed. We appreciate that our ability

to survive hundreds of diseases that decimated populations before us is a consequence of this immunity that has been transmitted to us through the blood of our parents. Again, this serves an analogy for another of the functions of education. In addition to the bringing forth of identity and transmitting the legacy of competence, education must also transmit many of the acquired immunities that have been learned by earlier generations and their exposure to a variety of intellectual and social diseases. (p. 9)

One must not mistake the knowledge of self to mean simply an individual identity but rather one that is tied to a holistic identity that transcends the individual, eventually leading to knowledge of self and others. The idea of self is not a new concept in education; as Pinar (2004) mentions, the fact that Dewey "insisted that educational experience provided a bridge between 'self' and 'society,' between self-realization and democratization" (p. 17). The threat to white dominance can be seen in this idea. A true understanding of self in relation to others would help African Americans see what "white America" (the white ruling class in America) has made them (I make a special note here to mention "white America" as opposed to "white people"). To understand the relationship between self and others is the political act of mis-education that white America continues to enforce upon African Americans. This has contributed to some major misunderstandings by the masses of people regarding the need for knowledge of self. Karenga, one of the leading proponents of black studies, has termed what is called *Kawaida theory* as way of exploring the knowledge of self.

Karenga (2002) describes Kawaida theory as "a theory of cultural and social change which has as one of its main propositions the contention that the solution to the problems of black life demand critiques and corrections in seven basic areas of culture" (p. 26). Those seven areas are the major components of Black Studies (history, religion, economics, sociology, politics, creative production, and psychology). Kawaida theory is the knowledge of an individual's past, present, and future possibilities. Understanding the past, present, and future possibilities gives inspiration and motivation propelling one to tap into their creative thinking (Karenga, 2002). The major premise of Kawaida is, "Know thyself."

Kawaida theory is an essential component for African Americans in the process of developing a true self-concept. Karenga (2002) notes, "A people whose achievements are minor or whose knowledge of its history and the possibilities it suggests is deficient, develops a self consciousness of similar characteristics" (p. 70). Elijah Muhammad clearly articulated the need for knowledge of self. Muhammad pointed out that the number one problem affecting African Americans was their lack of knowledge of self. His ideas about knowledge of self went far beyond the cotton fields of the South and the ancient pyramids in Egypt. For Muhammad, the knowledge of self is rooted in the originator, who created the heavens and the earth. Muhammad intertwined history, language, science, geography, and other disciplines to articulate the importance of knowledge of self. Ultimately, his ideas on knowledge of self and achievement went far beyond the current discussion about the achievement level of African Americans. His ideas were rooted in making gods; to be a god, one needs a superior knowledge. These ideas shocked the ruling class of whites, who understand the necessity of the knowledge of self. In fact, Gatto (2002) notes:

> It is high time we looked backwards to regain an educational philosophy that works. One I particularly like well has been a favorite of the ruling classes of Europe for thousands of years. I use as much of it as I can manage in my own teaching, as much, that is, as I can get away with, given the present institution of compulsory schooling. I think it works just as well for poor children as for rich ones. At the core of this elite system of education is the belief that self-knowledge is the only basis for true knowledge. (p. 30)

Elijah Muhammad used the knowledge of self as a way to enlighten, awaken, stimulate, and motivate some of the most downtrodden people in the society. He pointed out, "Knowledge of self makes you take on the great virtue of learning" (p. 39). His students demonstrate the awesome power of knowledge of self and its ability to inspire the search for knowledge. The ruling powers realize the importance of knowledge of self and have purposely created curricula around ideas and images that will put to death the real power of black thought.

In helping us to understand why the knowledge of self as it relates to African American children has not been implemented in a majority of the public schools, Muhammad and Freire provide insight into the purpose and function of ruler-sponsored schools. Elijah Muhammad directly addresses the purpose of the Euro-centered education in keeping the black mind asleep and the prospects of a new education:

> You should remember that the time of wisdom, now, is coming for you. And creative thoughts, now, are coming to you. And the God Who has chosen you to be His People will teach you and lead you how to fashion them into actual beings as the white man has done. Our creative thoughts were taken from us until he (the white man) rules his world under his own creative thoughts . . . We will be made a new people, for we have been destroyed mentally and physically by the teachers and guides of this world of the white race. Therefore in order to renew us (the once servitude slave and the now free slave of our enemy), we must have a new spirit that will produce ideas in us to become a new people. (1974, pp. 51, 131)

Freire (2000) notes that one of the major issues confronting schools is the technical nature in which they operate. According to him, students are simply receptacles, helpless beings into which teachers deposit information. This scenario is too often played out in schools that are predominantly African American. In many cases, schools are filled with teachers who have no knowledge of the historical reality of their students. Freire argues:

> [Teachers in schools that serve African Americans in poor school districts] . . . organize a process which already occurs spontaneously, to fill the students by making deposits of information which he or she considers to constitute true knowledge . . . Translated into practice, this concept is well suited to the purposes of the oppressors, whose tranquility rests on how well people fit the world that the oppressors have created, and how little they question it. (2000, p. 76)

Schooling thus remains a dictate from the higher-ups that is supposedly designed to make everyone equal. In believing this myth, the uncritical teacher assumes that African American students (because of their economic status, dress, language, and behavior) have arrived at this point because of their own shortcomings. This often leads to policies that make schools simply modern plantations with African American students being held hostage for several hours a day. In the controversy surrounding a black history program, one of the major issues of concern for students was the policies designed to keep them in subjugated spaces, negating praxis (Pitre, 2008).

Freire (2000) provides profound insight into the thinking of the oppressor consciousness and the oppression that exists in schools: "If they do not have more, it is because they are incompetent and lazy, and worst of all is their unjustifiable ingratitude toward the generous gestures of the dominant class. Precisely because they are ungrateful and envious, the oppressed are regarded as potential enemies who must be watched" (p. 59). This potential enemy threat has led many schools to have policeman housed on school grounds. In some schools that are predominantly African American, police officers and misguided educators resemble plantations with overseers. These negative stereotypes have not only led to oppressive school policies but have played a role in the self-helplessness that is felt by some African American students.

In some cases, African American students are likely to believe these negative self-concepts and contribute their shortcomings to some fault of their own. Freire describes this as *self-depreciation*, "which derives from their internalization of the opinion of the oppressors hold of them. So often they hear they are good for nothing, know nothing and are incapable of learning anything—that they are sick, lazy, and unproductive—that in the end they become convinced of their own unfitness" (p. 63). This might be a major cause for the violence that occurs both in the school and the larger community of African Americans.

Educators have often sought to address the issue of violence by simply looking at the African American student and his or her community background. There is no thought about examining the root cause of this violence. A key component to understanding the violence in inner-city schools can be summed up by examining how the oppressed who are shaped in violence display a dual consciousness. Fanon (1968) notes that "this is the period when the niggers beat each other up." Freire (2000) asserts that in many cases "to be" is "to be like the oppressor." This often leads to "the destruction of life—their own or that of their oppressed fellows." As a result of not understanding how they (oppressed people or African Americans) are shaped by historical legacy, they will tend to take out their frustrations on people who look like them, act like them, and behave like them. The saying that "a nigger ain't good for nothing" is translated for many students as, "If I am a nigger, and he is a nigger, then ain't nothing wrong with killing a nigger." This attitude is often reflected in the larger community and reinforced in schools where students have no voice. On any given day one can visit rural and urban schools and find African American students in pre-K walking with their hands behind their backs in a straight line to the cafeteria. Once the students are hoarded into the cafeteria, they are told by their teachers that they must be quiet, or else they will be punished severely. In the classrooms, the same kind activity takes place under a banking approach—teaching the test and not students, whereby African American children are silenced (put to death). Thus schools reflect a modern-day Willie Lynch mentality whereby the African American child is indoctrinated to believe that they should keep quiet because his or her thoughts mean nothing: *kill the mind, keep the body*. What are the possibilities when liberating education mixes with oppressive education?

Freire (2000) argues that "sooner or later, these contradictions may lead formerly passive students to turn against their domestication and attempt to domesticate reality" (p. 75). In the final analysis, students will begin to engage in a fight for their liberation. Freire states, "Students as they are increasingly posed with problems relating to themselves in the world and with the world, will feel increasingly challenged and obliged to respond to that challenge . . . Their response to the challenge evokes new challenges, followed by new understandings, and gradually the students come to regard themselves committed" (p. 81). Liberatory education is threatening to those who have an oppressor consciousness, whose ultimate aim is not to free but enslave. The following statement by Freire summarizes the challenge of education for freedom:

Education as the practice of freedom—as opposed to education as the practice of domination—denies that man is abstract, isolated, independent, and unattached from the world; it also denies that the world exists as a reality apart from the people. Authentic reflection considers neither abstract man nor the world without people, but people in their relations with the world. In these relations consciousness and world are simultaneously: consciousness neither precedes the world nor follows it. (p. 81)

Ultimately, the education of African American students must entail a curriculum that incorporates the knowledge of self. The knowledge of self connects students to each of the disciplines that they are studying. Farrakhan (1993) points out, "In the Muhammad University of Islam school system, our students' learning is facilitated because they identify with the subjects. They are taught they are the subjects. They are taught, 'I am chemistry'" (p. 49). It is easier for students to master the subjects once they realize that each of the disciplines of study is connected to the self.

In summary, problem-posing education is essential to the education of African American students. This means that education should also include problems to be solved. Some call this the *social meliorist theory*, whereby students are given contemporary problems that must be solved (Spring, 2006). Truly, a social meliorist approach might make the curriculum more relevant to the needs of African American students. Finally, we must rethink achievement. The brilliance of African American children is being diminished by the Euro-centered concept of achievement in the same way that success is based on the European concept of rugged individualism. To effectively educe the potential in African American children, achievement must go beyond high-stakes testing, disconnected curricula, and other limiting policies set forth in the No Child Left Behind Act. Ultimately, the education of African American children must be aligned with eternal principles rooted in the innate quest for knowledge.

REFERENCES

Akbar, N. (1998). *Know thy self*. Tallahassee, FL: Mind Productions.

Anyon, J. (1981). Social class and the hidden curriculum of work. *Curriculum Inquiry* 11(81), 27.

Comer, J. P. (1998). *Waiting for a miracle: Why schools can't solve our problems—And how we can*. New York: Plume.

Delpit, L. (1988). The silenced dialogue: Power and pedagogy in educating other people's children. *Harvard Educational Review* 58, 280–96.

Farrakhan, L. (1992). We must control the education of our children. Retrieved December 1, 2008 from www.finalcall.com/columns/mlf-education.html

———. (1993). *A torchlight for America*. Chicago: Final Call Publishing.

Fanon, F. (1968). *The wretched of the earth*. New York: Grove Press.

Freire, P. (2000). *Pedagogy of the oppressed*. New York: Continuum.

Gatto, J. (2002). *Dumbing us down: The hidden curriculum of compulsory schooling*. Gabriola, BC, Canada: New Society Publishers.

Hassan-El, K. (2007). *The Willie Lynch letter and the making of a slave*. Chicago: Lushena Books.

Hilliard, A. (2004). No mystery: Closing the achievement gap between African and excellence. In T. Perry, C. Steele, and A. G. Hilliard III (Eds.), *Young, gifted, and black: Promoting high achievement among African American students* (pp. 131–67). Boston: Beacon.

Karenga, M. (2002). *Introduction to black studies* (3rd ed.). Los Angeles: University of Sankore Press.

Kunjufu, K. (1985). *Countering the conspiracy to destroy black boys*. Chicago: African American Images.

McLaren, P. (2007). *Life in schools: An introduction to critical pedagogy in the foundations of education* (5th ed.). Boston: Allyn and Bacon.

Muhammad, E. (1965). *Message to the blackman in America*. Newport News, VA: United Brother Communication System.

———. (1973). *The fall of America*. Newport News, VA: United Brother Communication System.

———. (1974). *Our savior has arrived*. Chicago: Final Call Publishers.

Murrell, P. (2007). *Race, culture and schooling: Identities of achievement in multicultural urban schools*. New York: Taylor & Francis Group.

Personal communication. (2005).

Pinar, W. (2004). *What is curriculum theory?* Mahwah, NJ: Lawrence Erlbaum Associates.

Pitre, A., Pitre, E., and Ray, R. (2008). *The struggle for black history: Foundations for a critical black pedagogy in education*. Lanham, MD: University Press of America.

Shabazz, B. (1970). *Malcolm X on Afro-American history*. New York: Pathfinder Press.

Spring, J. (2006). *American education*. New York: McGraw Hill.

Woodson, C. G. (2008). *The mis-education of the Negro*. Drewryville, VA: Kha Books.

Part II

CURRICULUM

CHAPTER 4

Rethinking the Social Studies Curriculum for African American Students

RODRICK JENKINS

INTRODUCTION

This chapter examines rethinking social studies curriculum for African American students. The chapter highlights through case study an analysis of a comprehensive high school social studies curriculum using notions of pedagogy laid out in Paulo Freire's *Pedagogy of the Oppressed*. Freirean methodology is used as an alternative set of principles for creating an alternative social studies program that is more likely to offer African American students a deeper and more meaningful understanding of their own situation. The problem, as I will argue, is that some social studies curricula is designed in a manner that leaves students with a historical portrait of black people as inactive agents with respect to the historical process. In addition, the curriculum conceals the oppressive nature of social relations that make up society by presenting a narrative in which the underlying theme is social progress, which is entirely inconsistent with African Americans' historical experience and the exploitative and oppressive context in which they live. It thereby limits the possibility for students to become social change agents. This is the basis upon which I propose a social studies course modeled on Freire's notion of *praxis*—reflection and action upon the world in order to transform it. The alternative approach will be based on Freire's problem-posing concept of education that unveils oppression and presents it as a problem to be reflected upon.

The objective of the alternative approach is to empower African American students with a critical awareness necessary to take creative action for community and societal transformation. The first part of the discussion will focus on how Paulo Freire's methodology applies to the African American concrete situation and the African American mindset toward oppression. The focus here is on a description of African American students as it relates to Freire's conceptions of fatalism and self-depreciation. A case study of Louisiana's comprehensive social studies curriculum will be presented. The critique is historical in that it begins with the Hampton social studies model, which prompted the modern social studies movement (Watkins, 2001) and proceeds to a critique of Louisiana's present social studies curriculum. The chapter concludes with a discussion of the principles that will characterize this proposed alternative approach.

FREIRE'S PROBLEM-POSING METHODOLOGY

Freire (2000) explains that the pedagogy of the oppressed is a pedagogy that "makes oppression and its causes objects of reflection by the oppressed, (whether individuals or peoples)" (p. 48). At the heart of Freire's theory is the concrete reality of an oppressive social structure in which there are two poles: that of the oppressor and that of the oppressed. The principal problem is that the oppressed, being immersed in oppression and having internalized the views of the oppressor, cannot objectively understand that oppression (and its causes) and is thereby robbed of the ability to act in a transformative manner. Therefore, the oppressed is simultaneously the oppressor. Freire explains that "a pedagogy of the oppressed is an instrument for their critical discovery that both they and their oppressors are manifestations of dehumanization" (p. 48).

Freire maintains that the oppressed "must perceive the reality of oppression not as a closed world from which there is no exit, but as a limiting situation which they can transform." He observes that reflection or simply removing the veil is not enough for social transformation: "This perception is a necessary but not a sufficient condition for liberation; it must become the motivating force for liberating action . . . functionally, oppression is domesticating." In regard to the African American situation, this means that oppression functions by creating an obedient black populace that reproduces itself. Freire (2000) continues,

"To no longer be prey to its force, one must emerge from it and turn upon it. This can be done only by means of the *praxis*; reflection, and action upon the world in order to transform it" (p. 51).

When using Freire's method, one must understand the student's concrete situation, the implications regarding the African American collective understanding of social relations and oppression, and the psychological dispositions of African Americans in terms of fatalism and self-depreciation. First, the concrete reality of Africans and African Americans can be described as a reality of economic, political, and cultural subordination. Moreover, African Americans seem largely unconscious of historical-political-economic relations. As Freire explains, oppressed people are typically "divided between an identical past and present and a future without hope" (p. 173). The African American perception toward oppression can best be described as generally fatalistic. For Freire, fatalism is a limiting situation: "Until they concretely 'discover' their oppressor and in turn their own consciousness, they nearly always express fatalistic attitudes towards their situation" (p. 61). This keeps the oppressed from acting as historical beings by transforming society and reclaiming their humanity.

Horizontal violence is one of the key consequences of fatalism and is descriptive of many predominately black schools: "Chafing under the restrictions of this order, they often manifest a type of horizontal violence, striking out at their own comrades for the pettiest reasons" (Freire, 2000, p. 62). Moreover, this fatalism promotes a dependent feeling in the oppressed: "The oppressed feel like things owned by the oppressor. It leads to 'necrophilic' behavior: the destruction of life— their own or that of their oppressed fellows" (p. 65).

A front-page article in a Sunday edition of the *Baton Rouge Advocate* supports Freire's observation with respect to violence in East Baton Rouge Parish schools. Titled "School Violence: No One Knows How Safe Students Are," the article reports:

> The stories spring up every few weeks. A team of Baton Rouge boys ambush two New Orleans boys in a school bathroom. A mother comes to the principal's office to pick up her daughter, who's been in a fight, only to urge her daughter to hit the girl yet again. During class, a boy shows off a handgun to another student. ("School Violence," 2007)

Regardless of the article's intent, it evidences the need for critical pedagogy. Freire's methodology provides a way for students to confront the underlying causes of horizontal violence and subsequently refocus energy toward its eradication. In addition, Freire's problem-posing education fosters classroom relations characterized by cooperation and unity.

Another characteristic descriptive of African American students generally is low self-esteem, which is also contradictory to the objective of societal transformation. This low self-esteem is displayed in the hatred of blackness. Kenneth and Mamie Clark demonstrated this in their famous doll studies of the late 1930s. The Clarks found that black children, when presented with a black doll and white doll, preferred to play with the white doll and thought of the white doll as good and pretty and the black doll as bad and ugly (1939). Freire explains that low self-esteem is a characteristic of oppressed people as a whole: "Self-depreciation is another characteristic of the oppressed, which derives from their internalization of the opinion the oppressor holds of them . . . as long as this ambiguity persists, the oppressed are reluctant to resist, and totally lack confidence in themselves" (pp. 63–64).

Before discussing the present social studies curriculum, it is necessary to first explore Freire's distinction between the *banking* concept of education and the *problem-posing* concept of education in regard to their practices and their primary objectives. Freire (2000) explains that the banking concept serves the interests of the oppressor and hence inhibits critical and creative thinking: "Based on a mechanistic, static, naturalistic, spatialized view of consciousness, it transforms students into receiving objects. It attempts to control thinking and action, leads women and men to adjust to the world" (p. 77). This form of education is called the banking method due to the practice of "making deposits of information which he or she [the teacher] considers to constitute true knowledge" (p. 76). A primary characteristic of the banking method is that it is nondialogical: "Instead of communicating, the teacher issues communiqués and makes deposits which the students patiently receive, memorize, and repeat" (p. 72). Freire explains that the banking education aim is to keep students from critically considering reality and instead deals with "such vital questions as whether Roger gave green grass to the goat, and [insists] upon the importance of learning that, on the contrary, Roger gave green grass to the rabbit" (p. 74). Accordingly, the banking method of education "negates education and knowledge as the process of inquiry . . . It essentially facilitates the integration of students into society by fostering passivity [and] by mirroring the attitudes and practices found in society" (pp. 72–73).

Freire (2000) continues, "Whereas the banking method directly or indirectly reinforces men's fatalistic perception of their situation, the problem-posing method presents this very situation to them as a problem" (p. 85). The banking model veils reality, but the problem-posing model unveils reality through dialogue; hence, the banking model is antidialogical whereas the problem-posing model is by definition dialogical. Dialogue is essential if education is to be a practice of freedom. Additionally, banking education presents a static portrait of society whereas problem-posing education presents society as "a reality in process, in transformation" (p. 83). The distinction between the two models is at the heart of the critique that follows.

Louisiana's comprehensive social studies curriculum is based on the banking model. The principles of my proposed alternative approach are based on Freire's notion of a problem-solving education.

A CRITIQUE OF LOUISIANA'S COMPREHENSIVE SOCIAL STUDIES CURRICULUM

This critique of Louisiana's comprehensive social studies curriculum is based on the grounds that the curriculum denies the very existence of an oppressive reality. In other words, it presents a portrait of society that veils the unjust character of social relations. In so doing, the curriculum promotes oppression as opposed to liberation. The origins of the modern social studies curriculum (including Louisiana's comprehensive curriculum) can be traced to the Hampton social studies model (Watkins, 2001). The central role that the Hampton social studies model has played in the education of African Americans, as well as its role in the development of the modern social studies curriculum, makes it necessary that I begin my critique here.

The Hampton social studies curriculum consisted of five articles written by Thomas Jesse Jones and published in the *Southern Workman*, Hampton Institute's school paper, between 1904 and 1906. At the time of publication, Jones was the social studies professor and he later became the chairman of the Committee on Social Science, which was commissioned by the federal government in 1912. Soon thereafter, Jones became committee chair and the name was changed to the Committee on Social Studies. This name change had implications regarding the outlook and aim of the committee. According to Watkins, "Jones's conception of citizenship education became the consensus view of the Committee on Social Studies, and ultimately his ideas became an ideological cornerstone for the broader social studies movement" (Watkins, 2001, p. 108).

The tendency to conceal oppression with a narrative about progress is evident in Jones's first article, "Social Studies in the Hampton Curriculum: Civics and Social Welfare." Anderson (1988) explains that the theme of Hampton history courses was the "evolution of the races" and was designed to promote in black students "a new notion of race" based on blacks' alleged misconception regarding the nature of race relations. Jones claimed that black people's understanding of social relations was unnatural due to the fact that blacks felt that black subordination was unjust and unnatural: "Their acquaintance with the race problem has made them precocious in their knowledge of social forces controlling and limiting the development of races . . . while the colored youth is more conscious of social forces than the white, his views are not natural." Jones explicitly states the aim of Hampton social studies regarding black people: "Instead of regarding the difficulties of his race as the oppression of a weaker by the stronger, he interprets them as the natural difficulties which almost every race has been compelled to overcome in its upward movement" (Anderson 1988, pp. 51–52). Therefore, Jones would have us believe that slavery and colonization represent progress for Africans.

Watkins (2001) provides a useful analysis of the social studies lessons written by Jones and concludes that the Hampton model "was both a classroom curriculum and a statement of political philosophy which had the intent of teaching Blacks their place in a society in transition from agricultural slavery to mechanical industrialization . . . it was a treatise on politics, economics and the sociology of race" (p. 106). In regard to the ideological content regarding the role of education in society, Jones "believed that for schooling and other social institutions to be effective, they must understand the 'place' of black people. He relied on the classification scheme developed with his mentor Franklin Giddings to argue that rational and intellectual types (Anglos) should lead because the emotional and impulsive types (nonwhites) possess the potential to wreck society" (Watkins, 2001, pp. 47–48). Jones envisioned an education for blacks that mirrored the subservient position in the American capitalist industrial structure.

Likewise, Lybarger (1981) provides a useful analysis of the Committee of Social Studies seminal reports that, among other things, explores the social, political, and economic philosophy of its members. Lybarger concludes that Jones was attempting to design a social studies curriculum in effort to establish "the ideal American or Anglo-Saxon Character." He wrote, "In the minds of the members of the Committee on social studies, the 'improvement of the citizenship of the land' involved the cultivation of the virtues of obedience, courtesy, punctuality, honesty, self-control, industry and the like" (p. 82). In sum, "The good citizen was to be obedient rather than active, assertive, or demanding of societal and political participation. Accommodationism is promoted as desirable social behavior" (Watkins, 2001, pp. 108–9). In sum, Anderson, Watkins, and Lybarger reveal in their analyses that the objective of the Hampton model was to conform African Americans to oppressive reality and not to unveil that reality in order that it may be transformed. The impulse to veil oppression continues in present-day social studies curriculums in general and in Louisiana's social studies curriculum specifically.

Louisiana Social Studies

This section offers a critique focused on the world history section of Louisiana's comprehensive social studies curriculum. Other sections consist of world geography, free enterprise, civics, and U.S. history. This section provides the best example because it is only within this broader frame that the African diaspora can be understood in its entirety. The analysis reveals that, like Hampton social studies, Louisiana's world history curriculum veils oppression and depicts Africans as passive actors in the historical process and thereby limits the potential for social transformation. It too conceals oppression by presenting a narrative in which the underlying theme is progress. This is illustrated by the manner in which Africans and elite Europeans are depicted within the historical narrative in terms of both agency and oppression-progress. The world history section is divided into eight units: Exploration and Expansion (1450–1750); Renaissance, Reformation, and Scientific Revolution (1450–1750); Political Revolutions (1750–1914), the Industrial Revolution (1750–1914); Nations and Empires (1750–1914); Totalitarianism and Global Conflict (1900–1945); Changing World of Superpowers (1945–Present); and Contemporary World Trends and Issues (1945–Present).

1450–1750

The world history unit begins in 1450 with a section titled "Exploration and Expansion" (1450–1750). Hence, the history of Africa begins with the arrival of Europeans, which established the relationship between Europeans as explorers and Africans as objects of exploration and conquest. The earlier history of Africa is implied, however, when the period is characterized by progress. This is accomplished by focusing students' attention on technological advances that characterized the period. One activity, for example, required students to research and develop a timeline of "developments, inventions and discoveries" between 1450 and 1770.

Unit 2, titled "Renaissance, Reformation, and Scientific Revolution," covers the same time period (1450–1750) and elaborates on the theme of progress by focusing on "major developments in intellectual thought and the resulting political, social economic, artistic and religious changes in World regions" (Louisiana Comprehensive Social Studies Curriculum, p. 13). It is important to note that the major developments in "intellectual thought" had their origin in Europe. In addition, the unit fails to consider the role played by violence during the process of exploration and expansion. Also, no mention is made of the numerous instances in which Africans fought for freedom. Instead, the units effectively convey an image of a period that can be characterized as one of consensus and progress for all.

1750–1914

The next three units are titled "Political Revolution," "The Industrial Revolution," and "Nations and Empires," respectively, and each covers the period from 1750 until 1914. Unit 3 advances a political narrative in which progress is made as a consequence of the movement from monarchy to democracy. The change agents are all European philosophers and "the unit focuses on how major ideas of philosophers resulted in political revolutions throughout the world" (Louisiana, p. 21). The primary focus is on the American and French Revolutions, but there is no mention of the failure of both revolutions to improve the political situation of Africans with respect to slave trade and slavery. This must have been what Fredrick Douglass was thinking when he wrote the essay, "What is the Fourth of July to a Slave" (1852). It should be noted that it was none other than the fathers of the American Revolution who defined Africans as three-fifths human.

Unit 4, titled "The Industrial Revolutions," advances a political narrative in which progress is made from agriculturalism to industrialism. For example, one activity requires students to create a timeline that lists important inventors. Likewise, the agents of change were the "important" and mostly white inventors. Interestingly, one of the inventors mentioned was Eli Whitney. This serves as one example in which technological innovations could not be interpreted as progress for black people (or society for that matter). This can be said of all innovations in an oppressive society because all innovations were ultimately used to facilitate oppression. The unit focuses student attention away from oppression and onto progress with an activity that requires reflection upon working conditions at the beginning and end of the period. For instance, the activity requires students to reflect on working conditions during the early part of the period. Then students are required to

> investigate reform movements of the nineteenth century (e.g., child labor laws, rise of labor unions, prison reform, and public education). Then have students create signboards that they could have used as a part of a protest demonstration reflecting changes that these reform movements would bring about in the political and economic systems of the time (e.g., wages and price controls, extended voting rights). (Louisiana, p. 33)

Here it is worth mentioning that during this period, the overwhelming majority of black children could not attend school because they had to pick cotton. Additionally, black people were excluded from labor unions, and education was geared toward socializing blacks to accept a subservient position within the emerging industrial order (Anderson, 1988; Watkins, 2001).

The stated goal of unit 5, "Nations and Empires," is for students to "understand the motives, major events, and effects of Western European imperialism" (Louisiana, p. 35). Likewise, its major thrust is to create a rationale for the colonization process of the period. For example, one activity requires students to participate in a debate prompted by such statements as, "Spread of the industrial revolution led nations to expand their territorial holdings as a defensive strategy; strategic trading routes demanded possession of coaling stations and fortifications around the world; and pressure of growing populations alone was sufficient reason to open new lands for colonization and resources" (p. 52). These prompts divert student attention away from the brutality of colonization and onto justifications. Of course, no mention is made of Africans acting to resist colonizing efforts.

Unit 6, "Totalitarianism and Global Conflict," overlaps with the previous three units and covers 1900–1945. Like units 3, 4, and 5, its focus is on the "causes and effects" as opposed to the injustices. Political movements of colonized peoples during the era are not covered. In student activities, emphasis is placed on elite individuals that symbolize the era; for example, one activity titled "Meeting the Major Figures of the Great War" requires students to "prepare talking points for each of the following figures perspective relating to World War I: Schlieffen, Moltke, Joffre, Petain, Clemenceau, George, Wilson, Orlando William II, Nicholas II, Ferdinand" (p. 61). Another activity, "Enlightenment in the Twentieth Century," required students to research and describe the cultural contributions of one or more "important person(s)" in the following fields: Architecture—Louis Sullivan, Frank Lloyd Wright, Music—Louis Armstrong and Claude Debussy; Art—Picasso and Matisse, Science—Planck and Einstein, Literature—Steinbeck and Huxley, and film—D. W. Griffiths.

These six units effectively conceal the brutal nature of European imperialism from 1750 through 1945. In addition, the units collectively conceal the many acts of resistance throughout the African diaspora. No mention is made of the Haitian revolution, the numerous maroon communities that existed throughout the Western Hemisphere, the numerous slave revolts throughout the Western Hemisphere, the Underground Railroad, African resistance to slavery and colonization, the

Pan African movement, Caribbean resistance to colonization and slavery, or African American resistance to colonization.

Unit 7, "Changing World of Superpowers," covers 1945 to the present, focusing on the Cold War. Progress is presented by focusing on the rise of the Soviet Union and the Cold War, the merits of capitalism over communism, and the eventual fall of the Soviet Union. Like the other units, unit 7 focuses student attention on such elite individuals as Joseph Stalin, Harry Truman, George Marshall, Nikita Khrushchev, John Kennedy, Richard Nixon, Ronald Regan, Leonid Brezhnev, George H. W. Bush, and Mikhail Gorbachev. One activity requires students to compare ideologies in the Soviet Bloc and the "free world." I observed that the table used in this teaching sequence was consistent with Freire's (2000) contention that preserving the status quo requires that the oppressor deposits myths into the minds of the oppressed:

> For example the myth that the oppressive order is a "free society" . . . the myth that this order respects human rights and is therefore worthy of esteem . . . ; the myth of the equality of all individuals . . . the myth of the heroism of the oppressor classes as defenders of western Christian civilization . . . the myth that the dominant elites . . . promote the advancement of the people, so that the people, in a gesture of gratitude, should accept the words of the elites and be conformed to them; etc. (p. 140)

The activity effectively leaves students with the understanding that the capitalist system is superior to all other forms of economic organization imaginable and is not in need of transformation. Concerning Africa and agency, there is only one activity that is devoted even partially to Africa. In this activity African independence is reduced to nothing more than a list of dates. The role that African peoples played in ending colonialism is totally absent. The relevant activity requires students to "prepare three political maps of Africa for 1800, 1900, and 2000. The maps should indicate the growth of colonies and the emergence of new countries with dates of independence" (Louisiana, p. 55). To describe the situation of former colonies as "independent" conceals the real exploitive and oppressive character of relations between Western nations and Africa.

An interpretation of unit 8, "Contemporary World Trends and Issues (1945–Present)," is that it aims to create support for the wars being waged in the Middle East. Unit 8 is the first unit to focus specifically on the Middle East; therefore, the first instance in which students are able to think about Middle Eastern people as historical actors is in the present era. Whereas not one portion of a student activity is devoted specifically to the Middle East in units 1–7, unit 8 devotes 5 of 11 student activities partially or wholly to the region. One of the suggested activities requires teachers to ask students to "explain how religious fundamentalism may be partly responsible for . . . Taliban rule in Afghanistan, Shiite Muslim fundamentalists in Iran, and Shiite Muslims and other religious factions in Iran" (p. Louisiana, 61).

Another activity requires students to "describe causes and effects of terrorist activity, including the following: Chechnya and Russia, Kashmir (Indian-Pakistani conflict), Sri Lanka (Tamil Uprising), Kosovo-Serbia, World Trade Center (1993), and Twin Towers/Pentagon—9/11" (Louisiana, p. 93). In addition the students are required to write an essay with the following focus: "Why is terrorism so much more dangerous today? How is the availability of weapons a serious problem? How did the Cold War make weaponry so available to terrorists?" (Louisiana, p. 100). The problem with this activity is that it in no way implicates Western imperialism in global violence.

Unit 8 as a whole conceals the injustices of colonization imposed on Middle Eastern peoples and leaves students with an image of Middle Eastern peoples as terrorists. It is important that all American students realistically reflect on the war in the Middle East in order to both stop an inhumane war and to avoid being made inhuman by having to watch the war as if it were an episode of *M*A*S*H*.

In sum, the Louisiana comprehensive curriculum not only reflects a Euro-centered perspective that devalues African Americans, it is also directly connected to the type of instruction used in some schools that are predominantly African American.

PRINCIPLES FOR INSTRUCTION, CURRICULUM ORGANIZATION, AND STUDENT ACTIVITIES

Instruction

Freire (2000) believes that the principal problem the teacher must solve is that the teacher-student relationship tends to mirror the attitudes and practices of an oppressive society. In other words, the banking method is compatible with oppressive social relations. Freire explains that the banking method facilitates oppression through the following attitudes and practices:

1. the teacher teaches and the students are taught;
2. the teacher knows everything and the students know nothing;
3. the teacher thinks and the students are thought about;
4. the teacher disciplines and the students are disciplined;
5. the teacher chooses and enforces his choice, and the students comply;
6. the teacher acts and the students have the illusion of acting through the action of the teacher;
7. the teacher chooses the program content and the students (who were not consulted) adapt to it;
8. the teacher confuses the authority of knowledge with his own professional authority, which he sets in opposition to the freedom of the students; and
9. the teacher is the subject of the learning process, while the students are mere objects (p. 73).

A primary task that the teacher must undertake is to solve this problem. "The teacher is no longer merely the-one-who teaches, but one who is himself taught in dialogue with students . . ." (Freire, 2000, p. 80).This can be a difficult task due to students' prior domestication via banking education. The primary tool through which the problem is solved is through dialogue, which is central to the problem-posing education. Freire explains its relations to cognition: "Dialogical relations—indispensable to the capacity of cognitive actors to cooperate in perceiving the same cognizable object—are otherwise impossible" (pp. 79–80). This is the only way that teachers and students can understand how each is experiencing and perceiving reality. And finally, dialogue is the tool through which the instructor organizes both curriculum material and student activities and, in so doing, continues the process of unveiling reality.

Curriculum Material

Freire (2000) explains that the curriculum content should be arranged according to the *universal themes* of oppression; however, this can never be determined in advance: "The program content of education is . . . an organized, systematized, and developed 're-presentation' to individuals of the things about which they want to know more." Freire continues, "These views, impregnated with anxieties, doubts, hopes, or hopelessness, imply significant themes on the basis of which the program content of education can be built" (p. 93). For Freire, the reason that many educational plans fail is that they never consider students. Nevertheless, Freire explains that some fundamental themes may not come from dialogue with the students. He refers to these as *hinged themes* (p. 120). They serve the function of either connecting themes or illustrating the relationship between program content and student awareness. Hence, the themes that I list below are hinged themes—differentiated from what Freire calls *meaningful themes*, which emerge in the process of student-teacher dialogue.

Themes were selected for the course based on how they are related to oppression generally and African American oppression specifically. In addition, these themes are problems or major components of problems to be reflected upon and acted upon by students. The preselected themes are *critical understanding of African Diaspora history*, *critical understanding of black education history*, *critical understanding of racism*, *critical understanding of the media*, and *critical understanding of exploitation*. Books, newspaper and magazine articles, popular film, and educational documentaries were used as vehicles for reflection.

As mentioned, the meaningful themes will expand as a consequence of dialogue. Freire explains that as themes emerge from the thematic investigation they should be organized as a "thematic fan"; in other words, they should "open up in the direction of other themes" (p. 115). Freire provides examples of a number of resources that can be used "as long as [they are] carried out within a problem-posing rather than a banking approach to education" (p. 122), including photographs, film strips, posters, reading texts, magazine articles, newspapers, book chapters, and recorded interviews.

Student Activities

Student activities should be based on the themes discussed above as well as meaningful themes and should be reflective and dialogical in character. Both reflection and dialogue can be viewed as action and thereby constitute praxis if they are geared toward social transformation (pp. 128, 88). Both are important in the problem-posing model and are dialectically intertwined. The primary instrument to be used in all activities will be the reflective essay and class discussion. In each of the activities, students are to prepare a reflection essay focusing on a particular theme or problem. The essays should be read aloud during class for further class reflection and dialogue. Student activities are designed in order to raise questions and thereby facilitate the emergence of other themes, which becomes the basis for organizing curriculum material and student activities.

A strategy that Freire argues is indispensable is to allow students to analyze newspaper editorials following events. He explains that this nurtures students' sense of criticism when asked, "Why do different newspapers have such different interpretations of the same fact?" Freire (2000) explains that this exercise enables students to react to the media "not as passive objects . . . but rather as consciousnesses seeking to be free" (pp. 122–23).

Discussions should be focused both on the problem of oppression and our emerging understanding of problems. Freire explains that "all authentic education investigates thinking . . . by stimulating 'perceptions of the previous perceptions' and 'knowledge of previous knowledge,' decoding stimulates the appearance of a new perception and the development of new knowledge" (pp. 104, 109). Thus, it is essential that students reflect both on their concrete situation as well as their awareness of that situation. Student reflection essays are designed to externalize both. The dialogue that follows will be conducted in a manner that deepens the analysis begun in the reflection essays.

In summary, Louisiana's high school comprehensive social studies are irrelevant with regard to the African American situation.

This critique first began by discussing the Hampton social studies model, which is where the modern social studies movement found its origins (Watkins, 2001). It is here that the philosophical basis on which the present curriculum rests. I then examined the world history section of Louisiana's social studies curriculum and argued that it is designed in a manner that leaves students with a historical portrait of African Americans as being inactive in the historical process. The curriculum makes no mention either of Africans before the arrival of European "explorers" or of African liberation movements. This chapter highlights that curriculum conceals the exploitive and oppressive character of African American historical experiences since the arrival of European "explorers" on the shores of Africa. It does this by presenting a narrative in which the underlying theme is progress. It even fosters an understanding of slavery as being progress for Africans. Finally, based on a critical pedagogical analysis, the chapter presents an alternative set of principles for creating a social studies program that is more likely to provide African American students a deeper and more meaningful understanding of their own situation and in so doing empower them to be agents of social change.

REFERENCES

Anderson, J. (1988). *The education of blacks in the South 1860–1935*. Chapel Hill: University of North Carolina.

Clark, K., and Clark, M. (1939). The development of consciousness of self and the emergence of racial identity in Negro children. *Journal of Social Psychology* 10, 591–99.

Douglass, Fredrick. (1852). "What is the Fourth of July to a Slave." Retrieved January 2009 from www.freemaninstiture.com/douglass.htm.

Freire, P. (2000). *Pedagogy of the oppressed*. New York: Continuum.

Louisiana Comprehensive Social Studies Curriculum.

Lybarger, M. B. (1981). Origins of the social studies curriculum: 1865–1916. Unpublished doctoral dissertation, University of Wisconsin, Madison.

School violence: No one knows how safe students are. (2007, March 25). *The Baton Rouge Advocate*, 1–3.

Watkins, W. (2001). *The white architects of black education: Ideology and power in America, 1865–1954*. New York: Teacher's College Press.

CHAPTER 5

Increasing the Level of Mathematics Achievement in African American Male Adolescents

SHAHID MUHAMMAD

Imagine being asked to balance your checkbook, determine the interest on a car loan, or simply change from one currency to another. Are you extremely perplexed and stressed at the thought of it? Unfortunately and sadly, this is the daily dilemma of most Americans across the country. How many times have you asked someone how they are doing in their math class and they answer, "I never got that stuff when I was little," or "I hate math," or "I just wasn't born to be able to do math"?

Research shows that the average American is deficient in basic math skills. America at one time led the world in math and science literacy, but today has fallen behind so-called third world countries. Cuba has a higher math literacy rate than America and is considered less industrial and much poorer than the United States. According to Ladson-Billings (1997), the third *International Mathematics and Science Study* revealed that U.S. school children continue to lag behind students in other highly technological nations in mathematics and science achievement.

In our society it is unacceptable and frowned upon to be illiterate in terms of reading and writing; however, people in the United States openly brag about not having the necessary math skills to function properly. Ladson-Billings (1997) states: "It is acceptable in our society to be mathematically inept. Americans often matter of factly comment on their limited mathematics skills" (p. 697).

If the masses of Americans are suffering from math illiteracy, then the problem is chronic for African Americans, who have consistently shown deficiencies and shortcomings in their mathematical abilities and competencies. African American students are in a devastatingly terrible condition in relation to their mathematical achievement levels and their performances on tests of mathematical aptitude. Therefore, if the general population in America has math illiteracy likened to a cold, the African American student's condition would be more like cancer. Research consistently shows that the traditional methodologies used to instruct African American students in mathematics classrooms have failed them and are impotent in promoting successful learning outcomes for African Americans.

Ladson-Billings (1997) argues that despite the rhetoric of changes in mathematics teaching African American students continue to display poor mathematics performance. Part of the reason for the disparities may in part be due to poor teaching strategies and the cultural disconnect between mathematics and the African American students home language. Stinson (2006) points out in his article that the achievement gap between black and white students is most notable in the eighth grade. He argues that National Assessment of Education Progress data shows an increasing gap between black and white students and that the gap increased from 33 points in 1990 to 39 in 2000.

African American students are clearly not receiving the necessary mathematical instruction that will allow them to experience the same successes that their white counterparts experience. In addition to the gaps and poor performance the research bears witness to, African American students lag behind in the type and number of advanced mathematics courses they take and are consistently placed in non-college-level tracks that steer them away from the higher, more advanced math curriculums. According to Byrnes (2003) white students are more likely to take advanced courses in mathematics than minority students.

The educational reality for African American students is not a pretty picture. Several authors and researchers have cited and documented the inequities and deficiencies in the American educational system where African American youth are concerned. If mathematical literacy and competency were envisioned as a race, African American youth would be running the race with one leg. However, imagine all the inequities that research has documented and all of the difficulties African American youth are experiencing in attempting to master mathematics in U.S. public schools being combined with various other impediments, struggles, stresses, and problems.

What if, in addition to all this, a member of the African American adolescent group had problems with constant suspensions, constant expulsions, low self-esteem, high placement in special education classes, low track classes, and remedial classes? Imagine trying to master mathematics as an adolescent member of the African American group currently leading in the number of homicides in the United States or having the fastest-growing rate of suicide, or being the most targeted, despised, and rejected group of individuals in the country. This may sound farfetched and inconceivable, but this is the everyday reality and struggle of the African American male in the United States.

There is a multitude of research about the endangered species status of the African American male in America. The media bombards society with negative and degrading images of African American male adolescents that makes it nearly impossible for anyone of another culture or ethnic background to have anything positive to say or think about African American males. African American male youth are the most devastated males in the country. What are the chances of instilling and teaching high-level mathematics curriculum to an African American male when most Americans in general are having difficulty learning math and African American students in particular lag behind most of the nation?

Look at the statistics and data on the current state of African American males and we can see why some erroneously consider educating them a "mission impossible." Noguera (2008) points out that on reviewing the quality of life indicators, the African American male's quality of life is abysmal. African American males lead the nation in homicide, unemployment, incarceration, and have the fastest-growing rate of suicide. These issues clearly indicate the problems facing African Americans.

In the area of academics, Noguera (2008) provides clear evidence of the devastating condition of African American males in the educational system. He cogently argues that African American males lag behind their white counterparts on standardized exams, are overrepresented in special education, and have higher expulsion and suspensions than any other group. Noguera (2008) also cites the inequities African American males have to cope with on a daily basis in schools throughout the country. He writes:

In school, Black males are more likely to be labeled with behavior problems and as less intelligent even while they are still very young. Black males are also more likely to be punished with severity, even for minor offenses, for violating school rules and often without regard for their welfare. They are more likely to be excluded from rigorous classes and prevented from accessing educational opportunities that might otherwise support and encourage them. (p. 22)

It seems that society at large feels threatened by African American males, as evidenced by research on African American males in U.S. society (Bailey and Paisley, 2004). The list of researchers and scholars citing negative statistics, data, and findings on the plight of African American males is endless and gets to be extremely repetitive. However, it is clear from the research that a tremendous dilemma and perplexing impediment exists when it comes to attempting to teach math to African American male students. If African American students in general would be portrayed with the analogy of running a race with one leg, then the picture painted for African American males would be similar to running a race without any legs, blindfolded, and with hands tied.

Although the picture may seem bleak and the task to raise mathematical performance and achievement of African American male youth may seem impossible, there is hope and a light at the end of the tunnel. Part of the problem lies in researchers spending too much time painting the bleak picture and designing studies that examine symptoms opposed to looking at the root cause of structural inequalities in both school and society. Perhaps more studies should be done to illuminate those programs, methodologies, curricula, and models that have proven successful.

There are numerous programs, models, schools, and curricula all across this country that have produced successful and positive results with teaching African American students not only math, but also all subjects. One only needs to possess the desire and will to excavate the many cities and towns to find them. Noguera (2008) points out that it is possible to educate African American males. Citing a vast body of research on the learning styles of African American children, he argues that action can be taken to reverse the negative schooling experiences of African American students, particularly African American males.

Numerous scholars possess the tenacity and commitment to education that is needed to unearth those model programs and curricula that have been proven to work with students of color, particularly African American males. The question remains: what educational experiences, strategies, and methodologies can meet the needs of African American male adolescents? How can African American males learn and master a difficult subject such as math with so many obstacles, impediments, and shortcomings? Are there programs, models, and schools we can analyze to design the appropriate educational program to promote positive outcomes for African American males?

All of the above questions can be answered with a simple "yes" if one explores the current research on improving educational outcomes for African American males. There are many common themes interwoven in the research on academic achievement and African American adolescents. Here are some of the common themes one can decipher from the research:

1. A positive self-identity and self-concept are crucial to promoting academic success and increasing student motivation to learn.
2. A strong sense of racial pride and racial identity are necessary for increasing student performance in academic and social development.
3. A culturally relevant curriculum and teaching methodology is mandatory to promote successful learning outcomes for students of diverse cultural and ethnic backgrounds.
4. Positive role models, parent involvement, and specially designed afterschool programs have shown to assist in raising the academic and social development of black boys.

Because the nature of the dilemma concerning teaching mathematics to African American males is so complex and multifaceted, it would take several writings to cover all the variables and factors that scholars and researchers have examined. Here are just a few of the myriad research findings and studies dealing with methods, strategies, and programs that can serve to increase the academic performance of African American males in general and the mathematical literacy and competency of African American males in particular.

In Byrnes's 2003 study, an analysis of the National Assessment of Educational Progress to gain insight into what factors affect the math achievement of white, black, and Hispanic twelfth graders, researchers found that the following factors had the greatest predictive power on academic performance: parent education, high school program, coursework, calculator usage, worksheet frequency ability, liking math, and beliefs about the nature of math. It is interesting to note that all of the factors noted by Byrnes were qualitative-type factors independent of the student's cognitive abilities.

Most educators and psychologists know that a connection and correlation exist between a person's performance and motivation to do a task and their level of self-esteem and self-concept. One has to wonder why more programs and strategies that serve to promote more positive self-concepts and self-esteem in African American males are not utilized and implemented on a more massive scale. Justice, Lindsey, and Morrow (1999) suggest that any program designed to increase academic and social development of African American males must include components that boost self-esteem and promote a healthy self-concept. The results of their study on African American preschoolers showed positive correlation between self-concept and self-esteem with academic achievement. Their study also analyzed the effects of maternal education and the length of time the child participated in the Head Start program on academic achievement. The results suggested a correlation exists there also.

One of the limitations of this study involves the method in which the examiner acquired self-concept and self-esteem ratings from preschool children. Instead of using some formal method or measuring tool, examiners chose to use a self-reporting assessment, where the preschoolers basically assessed their own levels of self-concept and self-esteem. This may not have been the best or most efficient method, as one has to question a preschooler's accuracy in rating themselves.

Even in light of this limitation, the study shed light on how and when children arrive at a sense of racial identity, and this bears witness to the common themes of the research in this area that suggest improving

self-esteem and self-concept can serve to improve academic performance of African American adolescents in general, and African American males in particular.

Another common theme found in current research on African American male adolescents is the perception and motivation to learn. Many
African American males do not see value or benefit from being academically strong and, therefore, do not focus time and energy toward
academic pursuits. In addition to not having the necessary perspective
that education can lead to success, many African American males perceive intellectual and scholastic achievement as something that is not
related to strength and does not give them prestige in and among their
peers.

The prevalence of negative images and statistics of African American males, in particular, does not provide the necessary motivation and
inspiration they need to feel positive about their abilities in school. The
media and school administrators many times flood society with negative statistics of so-called minority students in regards to academic
achievement and test scores. Students of color are constantly told,
whether directly or indirectly, that their potential and abilities are far
below those of their white counterparts. This flooding of propaganda
produces what Steele (1992, 1997) refers to as *stereotype threat.*

Osborne (2001) points out that Steele's concept was used to explain
the underperformance of so-called disadvantaged groups—racial minorities and girls and women taking courses in "traditionally male"
dominant subjects like math, computers, and engineering. Steele uses
the stereotype-threat theory to rationalize why when all other factors
are stable and equalized, minorities and females still perform below
the levels of white male and Asian students. Steele points out that negative stereotypes of minority groups and females' intellectual ability
causes these groups stress and anxiety, which then produces poor performance.

Unfortunately, too many scholars and examiners are too focused on
test scores and achievement gaps among African American males and
their white counterparts to even consider external factors and variables
such as anxiety, stress, and other emotional impediments. The mastery
of mathematics requires a learning atmosphere and environment that is
conducive to the promotion of critical thinking and reasoning skills.

Could it be that some students, African American males in particular, are exposed to learning environments that cause stress and anxiety, therefore decreasing their ability to grasp abstract and complex concepts found in most math courses?

Osborne (2001) found that those minority students who were tested experienced more anxiety and stress and performed at lower achievement levels than white students, who had lower levels of anxiety when taking tests and scored significantly higher.

Zand and Thomson (2005) concluded that African American students' sense of self-worth affected their views of their own leadership qualities, which in turn had positive effects on their school bonding and ultimately led to reports of higher academic achievement. This suggests that educators can maximize student potential by investigating ways to increase students' perceptions of their own abilities and by creating environments where school bonding occurs in a positive and productive manner.

African American male adolescents need educational experiences and pedagogies that serve to increase their sense of racial pride and self-esteem. A study by Chavous, Bernat, Schmeelk-Cone, Caldwell, Kohn-Wood, and Zimmerman (2003) found that those students who possessed group pride had positive feelings about school and positive self-perceptions around academics. Additionally, evidence supported the fact that having positive group feelings along with high race centrality and an awareness of societal biases against African Americans may have a very positive effect on academic outcomes.

Research aimed at investigating the positive and successful models of education and strategies that promote higher achievement levels with African American students in general and African American male students in particular represent a breath of fresh air or a cool drink on a hot summer day. There are many models, programs, methodologies, and strategies being used in cities and towns all over this country that rarely get the public attention they deserve. Too many times, negative statistics and news about African American adolescents get major news coverage, whereas those short but powerful stories of success get brushed aside.

Stinson (2006) conducted a qualitative research study to understand the success stories of four African American males. In his research,

Stinson engaged the students in a review of comments other African American students had previously made on their schooling experiences. The study concluded that society seems to place more focus and attention on the discourses of rejection and deficiency than the discourse of achievement.

Not only does society seem to dismiss the examples of positive academic performances and achievement for African American students, but they also disregard the crucial aspect of culture and its relation to learning. Because white students seem to be outperforming students of color it is imperative that educators and scholars grasp a deeper understanding of multicultural education. The multicultural education movement is on the rise and many educators are rethinking the significance that culturally relevant curriculum has on student achievement. It is very obvious that students of color have a variety of cultural experiences that differ from the dominant white culture. If these differences are not addressed in education, students of color are neither gaining a truly just educational experience, nor are their needs being met.

Ladson-Billings (1997) points out that traditional methodology and modes of teaching math are crucial components of the problem. Teachers are ill trained and unprepared in math education and the method of teaching, culturally, is catered toward the learning styles and experiences of one segment of society. As traditional teaching of math in most schools reflects and caters to middle-class dominant culture, the cultural expression of African Americans is missing and misrepresented in school math. The presentation of mathematics is void of the everyday experiences and relevant cultural connections of African American students in particular, but of most cultural groups in general.

Ladson-Billings' (1997) article presents some positive techniques and strategies of one very successful math teacher. The themes and principles found in the article are very similar and congruent with those found in other research. The teacher in Ladson-Billings' study was successful in implementing some basic pedagogical requirements when working with students of color, particularly African American males students: she held high expectations, had a fast-paced interactive classroom, pushed her students to do their best, challenged them with higher-level mathematics and critical thinking opportunities, and she developed a positive identification with the students and their culture.

Another study echoed Ladson-Billings' (1997) sentiments in regard to what increases the academic achievement levels of African American adolescents and what methodologies and strategies have proven successful. Bailey and Paisley (2004) offer a very comprehensive collection of successful models and programs. They discuss a positive initiative in Milwaukee, where a special curriculum for African American male youths was introduced in Milwaukee public schools. The school district set aside an elementary and a middle school as special African Immersion Schools, where the culture and history of African Americans was infused into the general subjects and curriculum. Other programs incorporated enrichment components during after-school hours, weekends, and summer, where African American history, empowerment strategies, and positive self-identify curriculums were given to the youth. The programs also utilized African American mentoring, counseling, and tutorial sessions. Some of the successful models also integrated a community service component as well as parental involvement.

The highlight of the Bailey and Paisley research was their investigation of a very successful program for African American male youths, titled, "Project: Gentlemen on the Move" (PGOTM). The model project PGOTM is both developmental and comprehensive in nature. It identifies where each participant is academically and socially, compares this data with where they should be, and then formulates programs and activities to maximize youth potential. The model utilizes a holistic approach for the development of each African American male by addressing the many social, academic, and domestic aspects of their lives. Leadership and commitment to the African American community is stimulated through mandatory community service projects. Parental involvement and responsibility is another crucial component of this project. Project administrators reported very positive career and professional outcomes for those students who participated and that overall the project demonstrated tremendous success.

A number of research studies illuminate that African American males can achieve and succeed in academics in general, but in mathematics in particular. There exist numerous other accounts of success stories and personal testimonies that demonstrate the fact that African American males have the capability and potential to excel in academic pursuits and. hence, excel in mathematics. However, more research needs to be conducted to elucidate these success stories so they can be analyzed and their results replicated across this nation.

Questions and concerns still remain based upon the nature of some of these research studies. Many of the current research limits the academic achievement variable to simply observing test scores or GPAs, but rarely do any of the studies deal specifically with how to raise mathematical literacy and competency of African American male students. If the desire is to improve the performance of African American students and male students in particular, why does there seem to be so few studies that inculcate common themes, practices, methodologies, and programs that have shown positive results? What if a program or curricula were created that integrated all the common threads of success that exist in current research? Would we see results on a grander scale?

In addition to these questions, scholars also need to investigate whether the various differences in the backgrounds of the African American male adolescents studied has an effect on the results. How does the need for the overall reform of mathematics education in American public schools relate to the reforms needed to produce successful outcomes in math education for African American students in general and African American male students in particular?

Another area of concern is in the assessment tools and devices that researchers utilized to test things like racial identity, self-concept, and self-identity. How reliable were these various assessment tools and devices? Could new assessment tools and devices be developed that are more in line with the times and more realistic to current conditions and environments our youths are exposed to?

There are many studies highlighting the negative effects of stereotypes and prejudices on the academic and social development of African American males. How valid are the assumptions that the mindsets of those perceiving African American male students with a negative and stereotypical eye will change or be altered by some external force or cause? Can we assume that a racist and stereotypical teacher, administrator, or counselor will mature enough in moral development and racial-identity level to view and treat African American males in a more positive light? Should studies be conducted on the effect of external forces and negative environments on the performance of African American male students in math or any other subject?

So many variables, conditions, and complexities are involved in the overall picture of working to increase the mathematical performance and literacy of African American male adolescents that one can become discombobulated and perplexed as to where to start and what variables to research. However, if one is truly committed, one only needs to become a research detective and comb the country searching for those wonderful stories, examples, and testimonials of success, progress, and hope when working with African American males. Let us as researchers accentuate the positive and eradicate the negative.

REFERENCES

Bailey, D., and Paisley, P. (2004). Developing and nurturing excellence in African American male adolescents. *Journal of Counseling & Development* 82, 10–17.

Byrnes, J. (2003). Factors predictive of mathematics achievement in white, black, and Hispanic 12th graders. *Journal of Educational Psychology* 95(2), 316–26.

Chavous, T., Bernat, D., Schmeelk-Cone, K., Caldwell, C., Kohn-Wood, L., and Zimmerman, M. (2003). Racial identity and academic attainment among African American adolescents. *Child Development* 74(4), 1076–90.

Justice, E. M., Lindsey, L. L., and Morrow, S. F. (1999). The relation of self-perceptions to achievement among African American preschoolers. *Journal of Black Psychology* 25(48), 48–60.

Ladson-Billings, G. (1997). It doesn't add up: African American students' mathematics achievement. *Journal for Research in Mathematics Education* 28(6), 697–708.

Noguera, P. (2008). *The trouble with black boys: And other reflections on race, equity, and the future of public education*. San Francisco: Jossey Bass.

Osborne, J. (2001). Testing stereotype threat: Does anxiety explain race and sex differences in achievement? *Contemporary Educational Psychology* 26, 291–310.

Steele, C. (1992). Race and the schooling of African Americans. *The Atlantic Monthly* No. 4, 68–78.

Steele, C. (1997). A threat in the air: How stereotypes shape intellectual identity and performance. *American Psychologist* 52, 613–29.

Stinson, D. (2006). African American male adolescents, schooling (and mathematics): Deficiency, rejection, and achievement. *Review of Educational Research* 76(4), 477–506.

Zand, D., and Thomson, N. (2005). Academic achievement among African American adolescents: Direct and indirect effects of demographic, individual, and contextual variables. *Journal of Black Psychology* 31, 352.

CHAPTER 6

Overrepresentation of African American Males in Special Education

An Examination of the Referral Process in the K–12 Public School Setting

ESROM PITRE

> We hold these truths to be self-evident, that all men are created equal, that they are endowed by their Creator with certain unalienable Rights; that among these are Life, Liberty, and the pursuit of Happiness.
>
> —United States Declaration of Independence

INTRODUCTION

Although part of the U.S. Declaration of Independence, the above statement also holds significance when discussing the purpose of special education and the overrepresentation of African American males in special education. This topic has been discussed and examined by many researchers from the perspective that the overrepresentation of African Americans is due to a variety of factors such as socioeconomic status, the flawed referral process, cultural differences, and teacher training (Patton, 1998; Kunjufu, 1985; Oswald, Coutinho, Best, and Singh, 1999; Harry and Anderson, 1995). This chapter will examine these and other related factors such as: (1) bias testing procedures; (2) racial discrimination; and (3) parents' knowledge of special education rights for the overrepresentation of African American males in special education programs.

The most important purpose of special education programs is to support and serve children with disabilities, and this aim should not to be used to separate students because of race, social class, or gender (Losen and Welner, 2001). In the United States, the first major law regarding the education of students with special needs was passed in 1975 and was called the *Education for All Handicapped Children Act or Public Law 94–142*. This law dictated that eligible students were to receive specialized training, tutoring, and extra attention from teachers, counselors, and other professional support staff (Losen and Welner, 2001). However, Losen and Welner noted that many students have experienced unnecessary isolation and have been confronted with fear, prejudice, and stigmatization. Individuals with Disabilities Education Act (IDEA) (1997) states, "Greater efforts are needed to prevent the intensification of problems connected to mislabeling and high dropout rates among minority students that are misclassified, segregated, or inadequately served. Special education can instead contribute to a denial of equality of opportunities with a devastating result in communities throughout the nation." However, inadequate and inappropriate referral, assessment, and evaluation procedures used either to refer students for possible inclusion in special education or to determine their placement in special education contribute greatly to the large number of African American male students in these programs (Artiles and Trent, 1994; Patton, 1998).

The issue of overrepresentation of African American males in special education programs continues to be a dilemma in American education and society. Since the inception of special education programs, African American males have been disproportionately placed in special education classes (Harry and Anderson, 1995). Lawsuits have been filed charging that placement of high numbers of African American males in special education classes has been a tool for resisting court-ordered desegregation. Harry and Anderson (1995) also noted patterns evident in special education classes throughout the United States: (1) African American males are overrepresented in all disability categories; (2) African American students between the ages of 6 and 21 are overrepresented in Emotional Disorder and Mental Retardation classifications; (3) African American males are overrepresented in all disability categories between the ages of 14–21; and (4) students labeled mentally retarded or emotionally disturbed are most likely to be served in separate classrooms or buildings. Once an African American child is labeled as having special educational, emotional, and behavioral needs, there is a huge strike against them when they enter the real world. The U.S. Department of Education's Office for Civil Rights (OCR) has gathered data that confirms the overrepresentation, underrepresentation, and misrepresentation of culturally and linguistically diverse students in special education classrooms since the 1970s.

African American male students have been systematically and effectively excluded from the benefits of numerous educational opportunities by being relegated to special education classrooms (Irvine, 1990). Irvine further states that this can be equated with educational apartheid because of factors such as: (1) school tracking of African American male students, (2) the high dropout rate for African Americans, (3) suspension and expulsion rates for African American males, and (4) lack of access to a quality education. Many researchers state that African Americans are overrepresented in two special education categories: mild mental disabilities and emotional-behavioral disabilities (Oswald, Coutinho, Best, and Singh, 1999). Grossman (1995) noted that "African American males are much more likely to be enrolled in special education programs for students with developmental disabilities, behavior disorders, emotional disturbances, and learning disabilities" (p. 8).

The overrepresentation of minority students in special education programs, including those designed for students with learning disabilities and the educable mentally retarded, has been plaguing school officials for the past three decades (Majhanovich and Majhanovich, 1993). The factors responsible for such disparity remain the source of much controversy; unfortunately, scholarly debate seems to have brought about little hope for a solution (William-Dixon, 1991). Currently, there are disproportionate numbers of African American male students in special education programs compared to their enrollment in general education classes. In studies of ethnic representation in special education, researchers fail to address the impact of gender on the probability of being identified as having mild mental retardation, but gender disproportionality in special education is well known (Parrish, 2002). More than 66 percent of all students with disabilities are males and for youths identified with mental retardation in secondary schools, approximately 58 percent are males (U.S. Department of Education, 1998). However, according to Halpern (1992), the reasons for gender disproportionality are not clear. Maturational and physiological differences and higher rates of disruptive behavior by boys have been proposed as explanations, but most scholars regard these insufficient to account for the extent of disproportionate representation (Phipps, 1982). The overrepresentation of African Americans in special education has been an issue for many years and has been well documented by education scholars.

THE OVERREPRESENTATION LITERATURE

Researchers are increasingly focusing their attention on the issue of overrepresentation of African Americans in special education and a growing body of literature is beginning to challenge the many explanations for this dilemma (Patton 1998; Gadsen, 2001; Hale, 2001; Watkins, Lewis, and Chou, 2001; Serwatka, Deering, and Grant, 1995). The U.S. Department of Education revealed in a 1993 study that African Americans represent 25 percent of the population in U.S. elementary and secondary school special education programs. An examination of this trend into the 1990s clearly demonstrates that this situation has, in fact, worsened. More recent literature suggests that minority students that would have been placed in classes for the learning disabled or educable mentally retarded in the 1970s and 1980s are now being inappropriately rendered to English as a Second Language (ESL) programs (Artiles and Trent, 1994; Majhanovich and Majhanovich, 1993). In 1992, the U.S. Department of Education concluded that the proportion of African American males in special education programs has continued to be larger than their representation in the general school population (U.S. Department of Education, cited in Artiles and Trent, 1994).

Flawed Referral Process

Gender bias in referral and assessment has also been suggested as a possible cause of this disparity (U.S. Department of Education, 1998). Teachers' opinions about a student's need for special services may be gender-biased because society places higher emphasis on the achievement of boys. Since the U.S. teaching force consists of predominantly white females and society holds lower expectations for girls, assessment measures may overlook disability conditions that are more prevalent in girls (U.S. Department of Education, 1998).

The purpose of the PL 94–142 Act was: (1) to assure that all handicapped children have free, appropriate public education that emphasizes special education and related services designed to meet their unique needs; (2) to ensure that the rights of handicapped children and their parents or guardians are protected; (3) to assist states and localities in providing for the education of all handicapped children; and (4) to assess and ensure the effectiveness of efforts to educate handicapped children (Education Act for All Handicapped Children, 1975). The concept of "free, appropriate public education" is defined as special education and related services that: (1) have been provided at public expense, under public supervision and direction, without charge; (2) meet the standards of the state educational agency; (3) include an appropriate preschool, elementary, or secondary school education in the state involved; and (4) are provided in conformity with the individualized education program required under the Education Act for All Handicapped Children (1975). In 1990 and 1997, this law was reauthorized and its name was changed to the Individuals with Disabilities Education Act (IDEA). IDEA requires school districts to provide assistive technology for special needs students and include them in regular classroom settings with nondisabled students at least once a day. This practice is often referred to as "inclusion" or "mainstreaming." A student being served in a special education program has to have at least one of the thirteen disabilities recognized by IDEA: (1) autism, (2) deaf-blindness, (3) deafness, (4) emotional disturbance, (5) hearing impairment, (6) mental retardation, (7) multiple disabilities, (8) orthopedic impairment, (9) other health impairment, (10) specific learning disability, (11) speech or language impairment, (12) traumatic brain injury, and (13) visual impairment including blindness (Individual with Disabilities Education Act of 1997).

The Individuals with Disabilities Education Act (IDEA) and its regulations require school districts to provide a free, appropriate public education (FAPE) to meet the unique needs of a child with a disability. In most states, eligible students aged 3 to 21 have a right to FAPE (Public Law 94–142). FAPE does not mean the best possible education is offered at public expense to the student. Courts have defined "appropriate education" as a basic floor of opportunity. In other words, while IDEA guarantees equal opportunity, it does not guarantee a specific level of achievement or even a regular high school diploma. Kunjufu (1985) noted that "African American male children are placed in special education as a result of insufficient assessment tools; teachers' failure to understand kids from their point of view, and because they are constantly compared to girls" (p. 17). Further, Kunjufu documented that "African American children are 17 percent of the public school children in this nation, but constitute 41 percent of the children placed in special education" (p. 17).

Teachers' Perceptions

Some educators responsible for teaching African American students are not aware of the cultural differences and backgrounds of African American students and therefore view these differences as a learning disability (Reschly, 1980). Researchers who question the practices that lead to this disproportionate and overrepresentation of African American students in particular types of special education classrooms suggest that this phenomenon may occur in part because of biased testing practices and because of the cultural differences of African American students and the way educators view these differences (Gilbert and Gay, 1985; Reschly, 1980). Educators must be aware of the cultural differences that manifest through intelligence testing and interactions in the classroom.

At the practitioner level, teachers and parent training are a problem. There is a lack of appropriate professional development of teachers, in regard to the placement of African American males in special education (Gillis-Olsion, 1986). Teachers' perceptions of culture-related identities and their manifestations in the classroom are especially relevant to school achievement by students (Gay, 2000). African American male students' chances for school achievement increase when they, like their non-African American schoolmates, experience education with teachers who understand their sociocultural knowledge and take into account cultural factors when designing, implementing, and evaluating instructions (Boykin and Bailey, 2000). Based on the literature, teachers' misunderstandings of and reactions to students' culturally conditioned behaviors can lead to school and social failure (Gollnick and Chinn, 2006; Kunjufu, 2005). Researchers have indicated that teachers' perceptions and lack of cultural responsiveness can result in student psychological discomfort and low achievement (Obiakor, 1999).

One of the dominant stereotypes held by white teachers concerning African American males is that they are hostile, angry, and prone to violence (Carby, 1998). Carby asserts that "The motion picture industry and the news media shape much of how [white America] perceives African American males" (p. 10). For example, the motion picture industry and the news media have taken the movement styles of African American males, such as their walking style, and presented them in a manner that invokes fear in the majority population (Carby, 1998). Carby noted that teachers lowered their expectations of academic abilities of African American students who spoke in what is referred to as "street slang." In contrast, teachers raised their expectations concerning the academic abilities of African American students who used Standard English in the classroom. Teachers have been noted to view behaviors that are culturally appropriate in students' families, among their peers, and in their communities as overly aggressive, inappropriate, negative, rude, intimidating, and threatening (Majors and Mancini-Billson, 1992). Teachers also might perceive the walking styles of African American adolescents as inappropriate behavior that compromises their success in the general education classroom (Irvine and Armento, 2001). Irvine and Armento further state that as diverse students become more tenacious in their efforts to maintain their cultural identity, teachers who are unfamiliar and inexperienced with student diversity often overreact and impose unenforceable rules, expectations, and prohibitions.

Parents' Knowledge of Special Education Rights

Gillis-Olsion (1986) asserts that the lack of education and misunderstanding of parents concerning acknowledging and understanding cultural differences by professionals plays a role in the pattern of low parental participation. Poor communication between professionals and parents has been documented as a reason why African American parents are not receiving appropriate services for their children who experience disabilities (Harrison, 1995). African American parents express that in the media one rarely sees examples of young African American males who are achieving academically, being rewarded for those achievements, and feeling good about being smart.

Cultural Differences

In African American families, the research has documented that young African American males are heavily influenced by the popular culture that discourages pride in high academic achievement, demands that young African American males present a tough image to the world, which creates a mental image for these young males to become involved in a world of crime and drugs. Serwatka, Deering, and Grant (1995) argue that because educators have a limited knowledge of African American culture their perception of African American students is stereotypical. Students from different cultural backgrounds, and African American males in particular, may be placed in special education programs simply because educators, administrators, and professionals are predisposed to see them as problematic (Cuban, 1989).

Some educators responsible for teaching African American students are not aware of the cultural differences and backgrounds represented and therefore view these differences as a learning disability (Reschly, 1980). Additionally, social factors like the individual and collective use of stereotypes and assumptions about marginalized groups also contribute to the intractability of overrepresentation (Steele, 1997).

The discussion on race focuses on the problems minorities are experiencing. These groups, particularly African Americans and Hispanics, are too often seen as a burden to society because of what they cost taxpayers rather than as groups that add to the economy and the social and cultural fabric of our society (Grief, Harbowski, and Maton, 1998). African Americans, and African American males in particular, who engage in certain behaviors that represent artifacts of their culture—such as language (Ebonics), movement patterns, and a certain appearance—have been found to be referred at greater rates for special education placement (Neal, McCray, and Webb-Johnson, 2001).

Economic Factors

Parents and educators may have an incentive for children placed in special education programs. For example, parents might put their children in special education programs to receive extra income from sources like social security or Medicaid or to pay bills, rent, and so forth. The

U.S. educational system is perhaps the direct contributor to the present predicament that African American males are facing due to their incentive gains (Johnson, 1997). Johnson states that public school systems are embracing these programs to receive more money. According to Johnson, these programs allow reimbursement to be used not only for special education costs but to increase overall spending. Johnson (1997) cited the $5 million to $10 million a year in reimbursement that the school and parents receive. Therefore, parents and educators place students in special education programs when they perhaps do not belong there simply for monetary gains (Johnson, 1997). Everybody has an incentive to expand special education, but nobody has an incentive to rush an audit in public school special education programs.

Implications

Recent data show that African Americans constitute a disproportionately large number of students in special education programs (Oswald, Coutinho, Best, and Singh, 1999; U.S. Department of Education, 1998; Neal, McCray, and Webb-Johnson, 2001; Harry, 1992; Patton, 1998). Approximately 75 percent of diagnoses of mild mental retardation are linked to various socioeconomic-related environmental contingencies. As a case in point, poor children are more likely than wealthier children to receive special education services (U.S. Department of Education, 1998). The *National Longitudinal Transition Study of Special Education Students* (NLTS), which tracked a nationally representative sample of over 8,000 secondary school-age special education students enrolled during the 1985–1986 school year found a disproportionately high representation of African American males (Harry and Anderson, 1995). The Office of Civil Rights' *Survey of Elementary and Secondary Schools* (1993) documented that African American males accounted for 8.23 percent of the total school enrollment nationally, but accounted for more than twice that percentage in the categories of Educable Mental Retardation (EMR), Specific Learning Disability (SLD), and Serious Emotional Disturbance (SED). African American children labeled in the lower categories of socioeconomic status are 2.3 times more likely to be identified by their teachers as having mental retardation than their white counterparts (Oswald, Coutinho, Best, and Singh, 1999).

For example, in San Francisco, approximately 29 percent of the student population was African American, while 66 percent of students in the (EMR) classroom were African American males (Harry and Anderson, 1995). In addition, the disability categories considered to be most susceptible to bias are EMR, SED, and SLD (Harry and Anderson, 1995). The causes most frequently offered to explain the bias of African American males include: (1) a lack of uniform identification procedures, (2) bias in the assessment instrument used in diagnosis, (3) the attendant problem of poverty, and (4) a general pattern of racial discrimination in society reflected in the school system (Serwatka et al., 1995).

RACIAL DISCRIMINATION IN SOCIETY REFLECTED IN SCHOOL SYSTEMS

Schools respond to and reflect the larger society; therefore, the education profession can also expect to find racism in schools and other instructions. Expressions of racism may be less common in schools today than in the past, but racism does not just exist when schools are legally segregated or racial epithets are used (Nieto, 2004). Nieto noted that racism and other forms of discrimination—particularly sexism, classism, ethnocentrism, and linguistic—have a long history in our schools and their effects are widespread and long-lasting. The larger the number of minority students in a school district, the greater the representation of minority students in special education (Harry, 1992). Large urban school districts are far more likely to have higher percentages of minority and poor children in special education than rural school districts (Patton, 1998). The evidence provided in the extant literature has documented that the referral process into special education should be reexamined.

CONCLUSION

The issue of overrepresentation of African Americans in special education programs, particularly within some regions and states in the country, is a concern for special education researchers (Artiles and Trent, 1994; Losen and Orfield, 2002) and the object of study by policy groups such as the Office of Civil Rights and the National Center for Education Statistics. There is evidence that higher proportions of African American male students are identified as having the high-incidence disabilities when compared with the proportions of white students identified (Parrish, 2002). For example, African American students are 2.88 times as likely as white students to be identified and placed in MR programs, 1.92 times as likely to be identified and placed in ED programs, and 1.32 times as likely to be identified and placed in SLD programs (Parrish, 2002).

The overrepresentation of African American males has been a problem since the inception of special education. African American males have been of concern for school officials for the past three decades (Majhanovich and Majhanovich, 1993). African American males are overrepresented in the penal system in the United States (United States Justice Department, 1998). Special education, as it is currently structured, contributes to African American males' endangered species status. However, when dealing with African American males, this country has been less than average in addressing the problem of overrepresentation in special education. Educators must be aware of the cultural differences that manifest themselves through intelligence testing and interactions in the classroom. Based on the information provided in the sections above such as flawed referral process, improved teacher training (understanding cultural differences), increased parental awareness, and better economic practices one can conclude that there is a problem with the overrepresentation of African American males in special education, and this problem cannot be ignored any longer. This dilemma of African American overrepresentation in special education will not be resolved until changes are made in the training of teachers, new culture-sensitive testing practices are developed, and black psychologists get more involved with the process for evaluation purposes.

REFERENCES

Artiles, A. J. (1998). The dilemma of difference: Enhancing the disproportional discourse with theory and context. *Journal of Special Education* 32, 32–36.

Artiles, A., and Trent, S. (1994). Overrepresentation of minority students in special education: A continuing debate. *Journal of Special Education* 27, 410–37.

Boykin, A. W., and Bailey, C. T. (2000). The role of cultural factors in school relevant cognitive functioning: Synthesis of findings on cultural context, cultural orientations, and individual differences. Washington, DC: Center for Research on Education of Student Placed At Risk.

Carby, H. V. (1998). *Race men*. Cambridge, MA: Harvard University Press.

Cuban, L. (1989). The at-risk label and the problem of school reform. *Phi Delta Kappen* 70, 780–801.

Education Act for All Handicapped Children, 1975.

Gadsen, V. (2001). Cultural discontinuity, race, gender, and the school experiences of children. In W. Watkins, J. Lewis, and V. Chou, (eds.), *Race and education: The roles of history and society in educating African American students*. Boston: Allyn & Bacon.

Gay, G. (2000). *Culturally responsive teaching*. New York: Teachers College Press.

Gilbert, S., and Gay, G. (1985). Improving the success in school of poor black children. *Phi Delta Kappen* 67, 133–38.

Gillis-Olsion, M. (1986). Strategies for interacting with black parents of handicapped children. *Negro Education Review* 37(1), 8–16.

Gollnick, D., and Chinn, P. (2006). *Multicultural education in a pluralistic society* (7th ed.). Upper Saddle River, NJ: Pearson Education.

Grossman, H. (1995). *Special education in a diverse society*. Boston: Allyn & Bacon.

Hale-Benson, J. E. (1986). *Black children: Their roots, culture, and learning styles*. Baltimore: John Hopkins University Press.

Halpern, D. F. (1992). *Sex difference in cognitive abilities* (2nd ed.). Hillsdale, NJ: Erlbaum.

Harrison, H. L. (1995). Strategies for increasing African American participation in the special education process. *Journal of Instructional Psychology* 22(3), 230.

Harry, B. (1992). Restructuring the participation of African American families in special education. *Exceptional Children* 59, 123–31.

Harry, B., and Anderson, H. (1995). The disproportionate placement of African American males in special education programs: A critique of the process. *Journal of Negro Education* 63, 602–19.

Individual with Disabilities Education Act, 1997.

Irvine, J. J. (1990). *Black students and school: Polities, practices, and prescriptions.* Westport, CT: Greenwood Press.

Irvine, J. J., and Armento, B. J. (2001). *Culturally responsive teaching: Lesson planning for elementary and middle grades*. Boston: McGraw-Hill.

Johnson, M. (1997, September 25). Schools use Medicaid to dodge revenue cap: Public is hit twice, critics say. *The Milwaukee Journal Sentinel*, p. A1.

Kunjufu, J. (1985). *Countering: The conspiracy to destroy black boys*. Chicago: African American Images.

Kunjufu, J. (2005). *Keeping black boys of special education*. Chicago: African American Images.

Losen, D., and Orfield, G. (2002). *Racial inequity in special education*. Cambridge, MA: Harvard Education Press.

Losen, D., and Welner, K. (2001). *Comprehensive legal responses to inappropriate and inadequate education services for minority children*. New York: Pergamon Press.

Majhanovich, S. E., and Majhanovich, L. D. (1993). Issues of assessment and placement of students from ethnic minority groups: An Ontario perspective. *Canadian Journal of Special Education 9*, 13–21.

Majors, R., and Mancini-Billson, J. (1992). *Cool pose: The dilemmas of black manhood in America*. New York: Simon and Schuster.

Neal, L. I., McCray, A. D., Webb-Johnson, G. (2001). Something in the way he moves: Teacher's perceptions of African American males. AERA Conference Presentation, April 12, 2001.

Nieto, S. (2004). *Affirming diversity: The sociopolitical context of multicultural education*. Upper Saddle River, NJ: Pearson.

Obiakor, F. E. (1999). Teacher expectation of minority exceptional learners: Impact on "accuracy" of self-concept. *Exceptional Children 66(1)*, 39–53.

Oswald, D. P., Coutinho, M. J., Best, A. M., and Singh, N. N. (1999). Ethnic representation in special education: The influence of school-related economic and demographic variables. *Journal of Special Education 32*:194–206.

Parrish, T. (2002). *Racial disparities in the identification, funding, and provision of special education*. Cambridge, MA: Harvard Education Press.

Patton, J. M (1998). The disproportionate representation of African Americans in special education: Looking behind the curtain for understanding and solutions. *The Journal of Special Education 32*, 1.

Phipps, P. M. (1982). The LD learner is often a boy—why? *Academic Therapy 17*, 425–30.

Reschly, D. (1980). *Nonbiased assessment*. Des Moines, IA: Department of Instruction.

Serwatka, T., Deering, S., and Grant, P. (1995). Disproportionate representation of African Americans in emotionally handicapped classes. *Journal of Black Studies 25*, 492–506.

Steele, C. M. (1997). A threat in the air: How stereotypes shape intellectual identity and performance. *American Psychologist* 35, 32.

United States Constitution. S–1400.

United States Department of Education (1998). *Twentieth annual report to Congress on implementation of the Individuals with Disabilities Education Act.* Washington, DC: ERIC Document Reproduction Service.

United States Department of Education, Office for Civil Rights (1993). *1990 elementary and secondary school civil rights survey: National summaries.* Washington, DC: DBSCorporation.

Valdés, K., Williamson, C., and Wagner, M. (1990). *The national longitudinal transition study of special education students, statistical almanac: Youth categorized as learning disabled.* Menlo Park, CA: Office of Educational Research and Improvement.

Watkins, W., Lewis, J., and Chou, V. (eds.). (2001). *Race and education: The roles of history and society in educating African American students.* Boston: Allyn & Bacon.

William-Dixon, R. (1991). Disproportionate mental retardation placement of minority students. *Reading Improvement* 28, 133–37.

Part III

EXPERIENCES: AFRICAN AMERICAN STUDENTS IN SCHOOL

CHAPTER 7

African American Males in Urban Schools

MICHELLE BARCONEY AND ABUL PITRE

INTRODUCTION

According to Mychal Wynn (1992), African American males are an endangered species. The 1990 U.S. Census Bureau reported that African American males have the highest unemployment rates, the highest incarceration rates, and the lowest high school graduation rates as a percentage of the population in the United States. Added to these negative statistics, the leading cause of death for African American males between 15 and 24 years of age is homicide. Nationwide, African American males represent 85 percent of all children in special education while comprising only 8 percent of all children in public schools. Rather than decreasing, these figures continue to grow at astronomical rates.

Kofi Lomotey (1990) underscores that the underachievement of African American males in public schools has been persistent, pervasive, and disproportionate. In American schools, African American males are more likely than other students to be placed in lower academic tracks and less likely to be in gifted or high academic tracks. Ferguson (2000) posits a pattern in the everyday practices of school systems across the United States in which the kids who are sent to jailhouses are disproportionately African American and male. Consciously and unconsciously, teachers and administrators prepare African American males to fail (Wynn, 1992). Teachers who view them as culturally disadvantaged, culturally deprived, or culturally deficient can irreparably damage the self-image of African American males (Banks, 2008; Nieto and Bode, 2008).

Lessons and teaching methods communicate the feelings of teachers and reinforce negative ideas about African American males being unable to become successful in the larger society. Unless methods and practices such as the banking-system method and reproductionist strategies are eliminated, African American males will continue to have necrophilic schooling experiences rather than biophilic ones. African American males are being forced to discard their culture and adopt European customs and values or else become misfits who end up victims of the European dominated educational system The issues confronting African American males raise serious questions concerning the need to restructure schools so that they are just and equitable for all students — particularly, African American males.

The problems that African American males experience in the educational system today are related to a combination of social, political, and economic factors as well as the inability of teachers and school systems to combine their efforts to properly educate the majority of African American males. In this chapter, we explore these factors in relation to the experiences of African American males in an urban school.

THE BANKING SYSTEM

Critical educational theorists have argued that schools reflect the inequalities and unjust practices of society (Freire, 2000; Giroux, 2001; McLaren, 2007). Paulo Freire (2000) confronts the issue of equity and justice in the structure of schools in his compelling work, *Pedagogy of the Oppressed*. Freire describes schools and the practices that take place in schools as indoctrinating oppressed people to believe their oppression is the result of pathologies that exist within their culture. In an interview with African American males in urban schools who were suspended, expelled, or retained, their responses mirrored Freire's theory of self-depreciation. One student commented:

I think by getting put out of school I feel that I'm a very strong Christian, so I feel that everything is done for a reason. The Lord works in mysterious ways and he used that as a wake up call for me saying, "You need to get on the right foot and this is what you need to do." My getting put out of school and seeing my mother cry because I got put in handcuffs to go to jail for something I thought was small. And then seeing my father cry, who is this big bad Army man to me, and seeing him cry because his older son is going to jail. Then my little brothers asking me about, you know, "Did you go to jail?" And it's like it just hit me and like, "This is not where you need to go, you're better than this."

This student, like several other students interviewed about their experiences in urban schools, initially had feelings of anger and dissatisfaction; however, these feelings shortly changed to remorse and submission. The African American males I interviewed seemed to have difficulty in understanding the historical, social, and political role of education in perpetuating oppressive structures. The students acknowledged that indeed discrimination and inequality exists in schools; however, they serve the purpose of preparing them for real world discrimination. The following student comment demonstrates the confusion of these African American males regarding the issue of racism and discrimination in school:

In high school, I started off doing pretty good, but there was a teacher at school who I feel was prejudiced, not against race, although she was Caucasian. It wasn't against race; it was against a particular skin color. And I was warned about it before I got into her class by some students, and by my cousin who previously had taken the class.

This coincides with Freire's ideas about students not being able to read the world, which makes schools sites of indoctrination. Indoctrination is usually implemented by the banking system of education (Freire, 2000), in which students are viewed as being helpless, passive, empty receptacles ready for deposits of knowledge by an all-knowing teacher. Thus, African American students are forced to memorize information that has no real world application, keeping them ignorant about underlying social structures that perpetuate inequality.

Freire (2000) argues, "The students, alienated like the slaves in the Hegelian dialect, accept their ignorance as justifying the teacher's existence but unlike the slave, they never discover that they educate the teacher" (p. 53). In the banking system, student experiences are unimportant because students are required to memorize and regurgitate knowledge the state sanctions, which is called *official knowledge*

(Freire, 2000; hooks, 1998, as cited in Florence, 1998). In so doing, students are reduced to objects of the learning process and not critically conscious subjects of the process. As objects, the students are made into "dead things" and not living, organic, alive, and alert subjects who emerge cognizant of their own awareness (Freire, 2000). From Paulo Freire's position, education is a mechanical act:

> Education thus becomes an act of depositing, in which the students are the depositories and the teacher is the depositor. Instead of communication, the teacher issues communiqués and makes deposits which the students patiently receive, memorize, and repeat . . . the scope of action allowed to the students extends only as far as receiving, filing, and storing deposits. They . . . have the opportunity to become collectors or cataloguers of the things they store. But in the last analysis, it is the people *themselves* who are filed away through the lack of creativity, transformation, and knowledge in this (at best) misguided system. (p. 53)

In order to better comprehend the educational experiences of African American males, both the curriculum influences and teacher ideologies and their influences on African American males' schooling experiences must be examined. Welch and Hodges (1997) contend that those from racially marginalized groups (particularly African American males) are in a system that has failed to meet their needs and has reduced them to a status characterized as "at risk" as witnessed by Ferguson (2000).

Ferguson (2000), in her ethnographic study of schoolboys, found that the problems experienced by African American males in schools manifest themselves as early as third grade. Contributing to this is the referral of African American males to special education by teachers who do not fully understand the day-to-day experiences of African American males. To put it more explicitly, teachers do not have a clue what it is like being a black male in a society so focused on maintaining its whiteness (Ferguson, 2000; Florence, 1998; Freire, 2000). Biggs (1992) declared that, as a result, graduation rates for African American males lag behind those of other groups. In addition, African American males are not being provided with the pedagogical and cultural enrichment needed to survive in today's technological society (Biggs, 1992; Ferguson, 2000; Florence, 1998; Freire, 2000).

Additionally, a pedagogical framework must be established for African American males to succeed. Needless to say, the public school system must also explore the identity issue facing African American males. Unfortunately, the defense of identity and dignity of African American males are often looked upon as student resistance (Ferguson, 2000). It also takes the form of open hostility, noncompliance with teachers' directives, failure to complete work, refusal to pay attention, sleeping in class, acting out so as to be put out of the room, fooling around, and so forth (Lipman, 1998; Ferguson, 2000; Wynn, 1992; Kunjufu, 1989).

Welch and Hodges (1997) contend that because schools serve as microcosms of the societies in which they exist (Ferguson, 2000; Watkins, Lewis, and Chou, 2001; Freire, 2000; Fromm, 1964; Giroux, 2001; hooks, 1994; Florence, 1998; Feinberg and Soltis, 1992) and, if the curriculum is designed to be fair to all, it must be ideologically pluralistic and acknowledge the social structural flaws in this society—namely, those that have maintained inadequacies due to race, class, and gender. Furthermore, the educational system would have to be effective in assisting poor, ethnic minority children—specifically, African American males—develop skills needed to overcome and correct what society considers their social structural flaws. Invariably, the solution to achieving this pluralistic curriculum has surfaced in the form of multicultural education, which leaves the responsibility for a change in race relations to classroom teachers (Watkins, Lewis, and Chou 2001; Banks, 2008; Giroux, 2001).

The first and major aspect to begin scrutiny is the public school curriculum, which lends itself to the banking system of education. The mainstream curriculum is viewed by some as being ideologically conditioned by notions of domination, prediction, control, and racism (Watkins, Lewis, and Chou, 2001). American public schooling and its curriculum have failed African Americans male students by not providing them with the cultural foundation for learning (Ogbu, 1997; Watkins, Lewis and Chou, 2001; Wynn, 1992). It has instead relied on negative, pathological theories regarding African American males. Theories such as being "underclass," "at risk," "culturally deficient," or "disadvantaged" are theoretical rationale for educational and curriculum policy making (Watkins, Lewis, and Chou, 2001).

Beverly Gordon (as cited in Watkins, Lewis, and Chou, 2001) has argued that African Americans do have a cultural knowledge that emanates from the "existential" condition. It is the cultural knowledge that manifests itself in "literary arts, dance, media, theology, athletics, music, cinema, etc." (p. 57). She articulates that this cultural knowledge is marginalized and the suppression of it in schooling denies students connectedness; it is this that allows education to become libratory for African American males.

Therefore, another critical place to begin scrutiny of practices for organizing cultures of learning to revise instructional practices, pedagogical decision making, and classroom interactional routines in ways that promote understanding of African American male students, is indisputably the public-school classroom (Polite and Davis, 1999; Wynn, 1992; Kunjufu, 1989).

More often than not, the behaviors and interactions of African American male students are misunderstood. This misunderstanding often leads to punitive practices regarding African American males that usually result in unnecessary suspension from school or incorrect referral and placement in special education classes.

Too often, African American males are referred to special education due to teacher bias toward gender and ethnicity (Naquin, 1998). According to Naquin (1998), it is a teacher's intuitive theories and beliefs that play a critical role in the decision to refer a student to special education—a decision that is often based on whether a teacher feels the student is difficult to teach or whether the teacher harbors the belief that his or her teaching cannot influence the student's outcome. Algozzine and Curran (1979) found naturally occurring student characteristics, such as ethnic background, gender, and socioeconomic status, to influence the formation of negative attitudes toward students. Of parallel salience is the fact that teachers initiate most referrals to special education, and it is a teacher's referral decision that is the most significant factor leading to the eventual placement of a student (Lopez-Reyna, Bay, and Patrikakow, 1996, as cited in Naquin, 1998).

This link is an overidentification phenomenon that is occurring whereby students—particularly African American males who might not necessarily require special education services—are excessively referred and ultimately placed in special education classes (Naquin, 1998).

The deleterious effects and lack of empirical evidence of the benefits of special education indicate that most students who enter never exit. African American males are disproportionately affected by these unrelentless statistics, which correlate with Biggs's (1992) research on the lagging graduation rates of African American males.

Teachers need to be more conscious of the dominant group's media-constructed images of African American males and how those images might shape attitudes and dispositions toward African American males. Teachers need to become familiar with the historical experiences of African Americans. Hopefully, this will allow teachers to develop realistically high expectations for academic performance. Teachers also need to acquire a deep understanding of the discourse routines and dynamics of the educational settings that African American males find themselves in (Biggs, 1992). African American males expressed how some teachers in their discourse were disrespectful:

- You know if you're light [skinned], she's going to give you a "C" and she's going to pass you and things like that and I'm a darker complexion so I kind of fell in the back. But she was just prejudiced toward a certain color because it was an urban school. Basically all of New Orleans Public School for the most part is all black if not 98 or 90 percent black. Therefore, she pretty much had no choice but to work with black people, but there was a very few of us that were of the darker complexion. Even with us those darker people still had problems. Darker males actually; it wasn't any females.

- School is kind of like a struggle for me, because I be having teachers trying to let me down. I don't know if it's them trying to motivate me to make me feel better about myself. Like one of my teachers, um . . . they'll try to like, you know, say something bad about me or bring me down and I'll just pay them no mind and do what I have to do. They want to make me feel like I'm not a better person, that I'm better than that. Make me want to do better.

- They [teachers] either had to say something about me not doing the work, or not putting my shirt in my pants and not obeying the class rules and stuff because the teacher like . . . I had this Math class and he would always make me go to the board to work problems out, you know, to try and embarrass me in front the class and I just didn't feel like going to class that day because I felt like I was going to get embarrassed at the time.

• The teacher that I had in my first period class—I don't really want to say no name—but he tries to, like, play me like everybody say, "try to bring me down." So I just let what he say go through one ear and out the other. Like pressure, peer pressure, frustrations, and just all that put together, you know, just make me feel stronger as a person. Like I said, they try to pressure me and stuff, and bring me down and like, "ah . . . you can't do this; you can't do that."

According to Spencer (as cited in Watkins, Lewis, and Chou, 2001), African American males must deal with two types of negative social constructs: negative stereotypes of male adolescence and the hidden agenda of those who view them as inferior. Spencer contends that the schools African American males attend have been underfunded, inadequately staffed, and provided with a curriculum that does not meet their needs. Of utmost consideration is that African Americans were separated from their cultural roots and were therefore left in the position of measuring themselves against standards that are not their own (Watkins, Lewis, and Chou, 2001). This no doubt further suggests that African American males fall short of the standards set by others—most specifically, classroom teachers.

It is no doubt that the cultural mismatch between students and teachers impair African American males from being equally successful as their white counterparts. Unfortunately, the cultural differences displayed by African American males are emphasized and can often be stigmatized as negative, particularly in the classroom where the cultural, behavioral, and academic differences exhibited by African American males are looked upon by teachers as deficits (Spencer, 2001, as cited in Watkins, Lewis, and Chou, 2001). It is therefore necessary that a pedagogical framework of culturally responsive instruction for African American males be composed (Polite and Davis, 1999).

Schools are primarily concerned with transmitting cultural and social values considered as "normal" (Mattson, 1985). "Normal" is considered by society to be appropriate, and schools can only put up with so much deviation from the norm (Mattson, 1985). As a result, the practices of school systems across the United States give rise to a racial and gendered pattern of punitive measures for African American males (Ferguson, 2000).

Incidentally, African American male punitive policies intersect with racist ideologies and the stigmatization of their cultural identities. An example of this is noted in a study done by Grant (as cited in Watkins, Lewis, and Chou, 2001) in which first-grade African American males were perceived by white teachers as threatening. This type of thinking often results in African American males being disproportionately suspended and assigned to behavior-disorder classes and excluded from school and from the core curriculum (Lipman, 1998). This contributes to low achievement and resistance to schooling and further stigmatizes and criminalizes African American male students, thereby verifying the need to control their behavior.

CONCLUSION

If the needs of African American males are going to be addressed in the public school system, educators need to begin investigating the attitudes, behaviors, and ideologies of those who make educational policy decisions. It is also important that teachers interested in being responsive to African American male students must recognize and capitalize on the frames within which African American males routinely operate. Consequently, teachers must organize positive settings in the classroom that contain activity-oriented lessons and community building rather than negative verbal discourse.

Finally, teachers and administrators should be educated about the cultural, behavioral, and learning styles of African American males. Classroom practices should incorporate the pedagogical practices, policies, and ideologies that are relevant and representative of African American males. This could start with the implementation of multicultural education using Banks' Model of Social Inquiry (Banks, 2008).

Schools and school districts should dialogue with students and parents to determine what they think are the best practices. If parents are not coming to the schools, then teachers and administrators must find other creative ways to engage parents. Issues and policies should be proposed that generate a commitment to social justice for African American males.

James Baldwin affirmed long ago that "history is not the past, history is the present, you and I are history, we carry our history, we live, our history. We are history." The problems African American males are facing today in the educational system are historical. Education should be reinvented to empower all people of all races, classes, and cultures— not just a select few that we deem "mainstream society."

REFERENCES

Algozzine, R., and Curran, T. J. (1979). Teachers' predictions of children's school success a function of their behavioral tolerances. *The Journal of Educational Research*, 72(6), 344–47.

Banks, J. A. (2008). *An introduction to multicultural education* (4th ed.). Needham Heights, MA: Allyn & Bacon.

Biggs, S. (1992). The plight of black males in American schools: Separation may not be the answer. *The Journal of Negro Education* 43(1–2), 11–16.

Feinberg, W., and Soltis, J. (1992). *School and society* (2nd ed.). New York: Teachers College Press.

Ferguson, A. (2000). *Bad boys: Public schools in the making of black masculinity*. Ann Arbor: University of Michigan Press.

Florence, N. (1998). *bell hooks' engaged pedagogy: A transgressive education for critical consciousness*. Westport, CT: Bergin & Garvey.

Freire, P. (2000). *Pedagogy of the oppressed* (New rev. 20th anniv. ed.). New York: Continuum Publishing Co.

Fromm, E. (1964). *The heart of man: Its genius for good and evil*. New York: Harper & Row.

Giroux, H. A. (2001). *Theory and resistance in education: A pedagogy for the opposition*. Boston: Bergin & Garvey.

hooks, b. (1994). *Teaching to transgression: Education as the practice of freedom*. New York: Routledge.

Kunjufu, J. (1989). *Critical issues in educating African American youth*. Chicago: African American Images.

Lipman, P. (1998). *Race, class and power in school restructuring*. Albany: State University of New York Press.

Lomotey, K. (1990). *Going to school. The African-American experience*. Albany: State University of New York Press.

Mattson, C. (1985). *Misfits in school: Creative divergent children*. R & E Pub.

McLaren, P. (2007). *Life in schools: An introduction to critical pedagogy in the foundations of education* (5th ed.). New York: Allyn & Bacon.

Naquin, G. M. (1998). A study of teachers' sense of efficacy, teacher characteristics, student problem type, and student characteristics on teachers' referral decisions of students for special education consideration. Dissertation, University of New Orleans.

Nieto, S., and Bode, P. (2008). *Affirming diversity: The socio-political context of multicultural education* (5th ed.). New York: Longman.

Ogbu, J. U. (1997). Understanding the school performance of urban African-Americans: Some essential background knowledge. In H. Walberg, O. Reyes, and R. Weissberg (Eds.). *Children and youth: Interdisciplinary perspectives* (pp. 190–222). London: Sage.

Polite, V., and Davis, J. E. (1999). *African-American males in school and society*. New York: Teachers College Press.

Watkins, W. H, Lewis, J. H., and Chou, V. (2001). *Race and education*. Needham Heights, MA: Allyn & Bacon.

Welch, O. M., and Hodges, C. R. (1997). *Standing outside on the inside: Black adolescents and the construction of academic identity*. Albany: State University of New York.

Wynn, M. (1992). *Empowering African-American males to succeed. A ten-step approach for parents and teachers*. Marietta, GA: Rising Sun Publishing.

CHAPTER 8

The Experiences of African American Males in Special Education

An Analysis of the Student Perspective

ESROM PITRE AND CHANCE LEWIS

INTRODUCTION

In this section, we discuss the experiences of African American males placed in special education. This is one of the few studies to document the experiences encountered by African American males placed in special education settings. A qualitative study was used to examine the experiences of African American males in special education Emotional Disorder (ED) programs in the K–12 public-school setting. The participants for this study were 10 African American high school males within an urban school district in the state of Louisiana that have spent a minimum of two years in special education ED classrooms. This study revealed three major themes for these African American males: (1) "I wanted to be somebody"; (2) "We've been had, we've been tricked. We've been bamboozled"; and (3) "They don't care about us." Based on these findings, recommendations were made for education professionals, parents, and school districts.

ANALYSIS OF THE STUDENT PERSPECTIVE

The purpose of special education and the overrepresentation of African American males in special education has been discussed and examined by numerous researchers from the perspective that the overrepresentation of African American males is due to a variety of factors, such as parents' knowledge of special education rights, the flawed referral process, racial discrimination, and teacher training (Harry and

Anderson, 1994; Kunjufu, 2005; Oswald, Coutinho, Best, and Singh, 1999; Patton, 1998).

Over the last several decades, there has been a concern that African American elementary and secondary students with disabilities are over-represented in special education placement even though these students do not meet the criteria of a handicapping condition as defined by law (Harry and Anderson, 1994). This concern has been found to be partic-ularly true for African American male students who are perceived to have more behavioral or disciplinary problems than their public-school counterparts. The struggles for equal education for African American students have historically been challenging (Irvine, 1990). Brown (2001) elaborates on this discussion when she described the failure of the American educational system for African American students:

> This can be equated with educational apartheid. Factors such as school tracking of African American students, drop out rates, suspension, ex-pulsion rates, lack of access to quality education and culturally inappro-priate and insensitive instruction vividly reveal a stark picture of abysmal conditions and mediocre education imposed upon African American children in educational programs. (p. 2)

In our society, young African American men are at a higher risk of being unemployed, being involved with the criminal justice system, and committing suicide (Watkins and Kurtz, 2001). Since the inception of special education, African American males have been overrepre-sented in special education programs, which is a direct cause of this population being overrepresented in the penal system in the United States (United States Justice Department, 1997). The overrepresenta-tion of African American male children and youth in special education programs for students with learning disabilities, severe emotional or behavioral disorders, and mental disabilities has remained a persistent reality in American public schools even after more than 20 years of recognition of this phenomenon (Artiles and Trent, 1994).

The overrepresentation of African American students, particularly African American males in special classes for learning disabilities (LD), mental retardation (MR), and emotional and behavioral disorders

(EBD), are prevalent in many school districts throughout the country (Kunjufu, 2005; Serwatka, Deering, and Grant, 1995). African American males are often placed in restrictive and self-contained classrooms rather than in classrooms for students with mild disabilities (Grant, 1992). National efforts to reduce the percentage of African American males in ED special education programs have failed (Chinn and Hughes, 1987; Oswald, Coutinho, Best, and Singh, 1999; Parrish, 2002). As a result of these decisions, a segment of American society is being denied appropriate services and opportunities to interact and acquire worthwhile social and educational values (Patton, 1998).

Several authors have made a convincing case that African American males in the United States are members of an "endangered species" (Gibbs, 1988; Irvine and York, 1993). As a case in point, African American students are 2.88 times as likely as white students to be identified and placed in MR programs, 1.92 times as likely to be identified and placed in ED programs, and 1.32 times as likely to be identified and placed in LD programs (Parrish, 2002). Patton (1998) states that in spite of all the studies and scripting of this issue, the proportion of African American males identified as mentally disabled has not changed much from 38 percent in 1975 when those students constituted 15 percent of the school population. In 1991, African American students made up approximately 16 percent of this nation's school population and 35 percent of the special education population (Harry and Anderson, 1994). In 2002, African American students comprised approximately 14 percent of the school population; however, they constituted almost 40 percent of the students in special education (Kunjufu, 2002). Further, it is well documented that African American males are particularly overrepresented both in disciplinary practices and in certain special education categories and typically receive their special education in segregated classrooms or buildings (Harry and Anderson, 1994).

The provisions of the Individuals with Disabilities Education Act of 1997 (IDEA) are intended to provide a free and appropriate public education (FAPE) to all students enrolled for special education services (IDEA, P.L. 105–17, 1997). However, in a 1995 report from the U.S. Department of Education, Congress did not find students from different ethnic and economically disadvantaged backgrounds to be equal with their white or economically advantaged peers. Instead, the combination of being poor, a minority, and from an urban environment put this demographic group at risk for education failure, inappropriate placement decisions, and poor educational outcomes (U.S. Department of Education, 1997).

THE OVERREPRESENTATION OF AFRICAN AMERICAN MALES IN SPECIAL EDUCATION

For more than three decades, both advocates and educators have been interested in the educational dilemma surrounding the overrepresentation of African American males in special education (Dunn, 1968; Hilliard, 1990). African American males are one-and-one-half times more likely to be labeled as emotionally disturbed (ED) than other non–African American students and are placed in special needs programs more frequently than their peers (Coutinho and Oswald, 1998; Harry, 1992). The overrepresentation and inappropriate placement of African American males is a concern at this time. The public concern remains that although America's student body is becoming more and more diverse, children who are nonwhite, nonnative English-speaking, or poor continue to be identified more frequently as having disabilities and to be served in more segregated placement than their peers (Artiles and Trent, 1994; Coutinho and Oswald, 1998).

The racial imbalance in special education has long been an issue for professional educators (Dunn, 1968). Dunn shocked the academic community when he criticized the discriminatory tendency regarding overrepresentation and placement of minority students in special education classrooms. Larson (1975) found that the race of a student was a significant determinant of teacher referrals to educable mentally retarded (ED) programs. In addition, he found that African American males were referred to ED significantly more often than Caucasian males. The literature has reported that if an African American child is placed in special education, 80 percent of the time the child will be male (Kunjufu, 2002). As a result, the overrepresentation of African American males in certain special education programs has been a persistent problem negatively affecting large numbers of African American families, the field of special education, and society at large.

The Stigma of the Special Education
Label on African American Males

Patton (1998) states that the sociopolitical and historical roots of the disproportionate representation problem addressed predate the field of special education, with origins as early as 1619. Willie, Garibaldi, and Reed (1991) state that unequal treatment can be traced back to the arrival of African Americans in the United States. Watkins and Kurtz (2001) document a variety of factors both at home and in school that contribute to African American young men's high-risk status. For example, more African American children are raised in poor, single-parent families than children of any other racial or ethnic group (Mincy, 1994). Approximately 50 percent of African American young men live below the poverty line and 42 percent live in single-parent households (Gibbs, 1988; Irvine and York, 1993).

African American children of single-parent homes are more likely than children from two-parent households to experience behavioral problems and to drop out of school; research indicates that these problems are exacerbated when the child is male (Mincy, 1994). This problem is expanded by the fact that many African American male youths today fail to receive a quality, life-enhancing education in precisely those special education programs in which they are often inappropriately placed (Heller, 1992; Hilliard, 1992). The special education label worn by these students often serves as a stigma, producing negative effects on the bearer of the label and others interacting with the stigmatized individual (Goffman, 1963).

In 2001, Rod Paige, Secretary of Education, testified to the following before Congress:

> For minority students, misclassification or inappropriate placement in special education programs can have significant adverse consequences. . . . The stigma of being misclassified as mentally retarded or seriously emotionally disturbed, or as having a behavioral disorder may also have serious consequences in terms of the student's self-perception and the

perception of others, including family, peers, teachers and future employers.

This limited exposure with the core academic curriculum continues the spiral of "lower levels of achievement, decreased likelihood of post secondary education and more limited employment" (Markowitz, Garcia, and Eichelberger, 1997, p. 3).

Concerns about racial discrimination and violations of civil rights are raised when African American youths are consistently misidentified and disproportionately placed in special education programs (Reschly, 1996). Reschly further states that African American males have traditionally been denied opportunities to excel in our society; disproportionately selecting them for special education placement appears to be a continuation of the practice of treating them as innately inferior, which is wrong by any standard and does not meet their need for a free and appropriate public education.

Overrepresentation in Emotional Disturbance Classrooms

A body of research on the overrepresentation of African American males in special education has been established (Artiles and Trent, 1994; Chinn and Hughes, 1987; Coutinho and Oswald, 1999; Dunn, 1968; Parrish, 2002). Currently, African American males are significantly overrepresented in classrooms for students with Emotional Disorder (ED) at a rate that is over one-and-one-half times more than their white peers (Oswald, Coutinho, Best, and Singh, 1999; Parrish, 2009). In figure 8.1, we see that

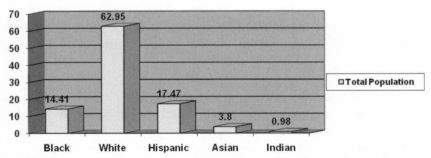

Figure 8.1. *National 2000 census population (percentage) for children ages 6–21 by race/ethnicity for the school year 2000–2001.*

during the 2000–2001 school year, African American-black students made up approximately 14.41 percent of the total U.S. elementary and secondary school population, while whites made up 62.95 percent, Hispanics 17.47 percent, Asians 3.8 percent, and Indians 0.98 percent. As we clearly see from these figures, African Americans are the third-largest ethnic group in U.S. elementary and secondary schools.

Figure 8.2 indicates the percentage of ethnic groups in ED programs across the United States in the 2000–2001 academic school year. African Americans represent approximately 26.65 percent, whites 62.6 percent, Asians 1.26 percent, Hispanics 8.12 percent, and Indians 1.23 percent. If we examine figure 8.2 closely, we find that the representation of African Americans (26.65 percent) in ED programs is nearly double their representation as students in U.S. elementary and secondary schools.

As a result of these shocking numbers, we continue to see the overrepresentation of African American males in special education. The issue of the overrepresentation of African American students in special education programs has continued to be one of those occurrences in education that only a few educators and other stakeholders adequately addressed. This problem has negative implications for these students' school performance and dropout rate. According to Oswald and colleagues (1999), "The dropout rate is 86 percent higher for African Americans than for Whites . . . with more than 50 percent of African Americans in large cities dropping out of school" (p. 23). As a result of this phenomenon, only a few scholars have ever discussed this issue with the population that is most affected: the African American male.

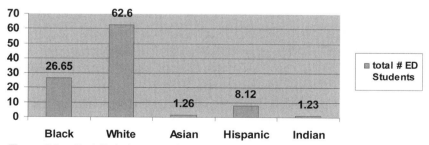

Figure 8.2. *Racial/ethnic composition percentage of students' (ages 6–21) emotional disturbance 2000–2001.*

METHODOLOGY

A qualitative research design utilizing retrospective interviews (Reiff, Gerber, and Ginsberg, 1997) was employed with ten African American male students in special education, emotionally disturbed programs in a predominately African American urban school district in southern Louisiana during the fall 2006 academic semester. All the African American males interviewed were in the eleventh and twelfth grades at two of the local high schools within the school district under study. The school district in southern Louisiana had a total of 46,910 students during the time of study, of which 75.8 percent were African American. Unfortunately, African American students comprised 68 percent of the total ED enrollment in the state of Louisiana. Further, each of the African American males who participated in this study had been enrolled in special education at their high schools for at least two years. Given this, the African American males in this special education program had enough experience in special education to make a determination about their educational environment.

The African American males who participated in this study were interviewed using an open-ended interview schedule of eleven questions. The questions were derived from the literature on African American student experiences in education, the impact of the overrepresentation of African American males in special education, and the career aspiration literature for high school students. The questions were focused on the students' backgrounds and their personal perceptions about being in special education, their experiences during a typical day in special education, their future career goals, and the impact of special education on these goals. Each interview was conducted in a face-to-face format, ranged from 90 minutes to over 2 hours, and sought to answer the following research questions: (1) What are the experiences of African American males in special education emotional disorder programs? and (2) What do African American males think about the type of education they are receiving in special education?

Data were analyzed after transcribing all interviews and coding them in the following phases: open coding, refinement of coding, and axial coding (Glaser, 1992). In the final phase, key themes and patterns were identified and developed that transcended each of the coding categories (Miles and Huberman, 1994). The key themes and patterns identified by the ten participants were not compared between participants in this study but were treated as one cohort group relating their experiences in their special education programs. Three key themes emerged from the analysis. Validity of the results was attained by applying Lincoln and Guba's (1985) notions of trustworthiness to the data collection process and findings.

FINDINGS

Three emergent themes characterized the responses of the experiences of the African American male students in this emotionally disturbed (ED) special education program. These themes included the following categories: "I wanted to be somebody"; "We've been tricked, we've been had, we've been bamboozled"; and "They don't care." These themes are developed below and following the discussion of the findings, recommendations are made to improve the experiences of African American males in emotionally disturbed special education settings and special education in general.

"I Wanted to Be Somebody."

One of the major themes for African American male students in this study was the notion that they "wanted to be somebody." For several students, big dreams and career aspirations were significantly stifled because they were "locked in" the special educational environment. It is a common perception by many in the school environment that African American males in special education do not care about their future. Surprisingly, many of the African American males in this study mentioned they had good grades prior to being placed in special education ED classrooms. The comments of several African American males in this study underscore the fact that they had great aspirations after high school but special education did not assist their dreams in becoming reality. For example, here are a few of the student comments that develop this theme:

- "I would like to take over Hollywood. I want to be an actor, start my own business, write books, and sing. First, I need to go to college to learn how to start my own business."

- "I would like to go to college and become an architect. I can design things and build things now. My biggest dream was to become an architect."
- "I really, really want to be a computer engineer or software builder. Every time a computer technician comes to school I ask [him] questions and he allows me to work on the computer. I can take the computer apart and put it back together."
- "I would like to go to college and then return to my school and help kids like me. I think I have the skills to reach students . . . I really think I could be a great teacher."
- "I would like to go to the Navy or Air Force Academy. I really want to become a pilot. If that doesn't work out, I would like to become an artist."
- "After high school, I would like to go to college and learn how to draw on the computer. I would like to use the computer to draw and work for Disney World."

Clearly, African American male participants in this study had a vision of what they wanted to do after high school. The majority of participants had dreams of going to college and starting a productive career. In other words, they wanted to be somebody, however, they eventually found out that their goals would be much harder to achieve because they did not receive an adequate education in the special education classroom. The students felt like they were cheated and their teachers did not adequately prepare them to do anything after high school.

"We've been had, we've been tricked. We've been bamboozled."

Along with the big dreams of African American male students in this study, many of the participants felt they were not given the correct information about special education. In other words, they felt that they, along with their parents, were tricked into pursuing special education as a viable academic option. The parents were misinformed about special education and the students were persuaded into staying in special education by getting snacks and being allowed to watch videos every day. Most of the participants thought they were being put in special education to get caught up with their school work. Note their comments below:

- "I was put in special education because they told my parents that I needed help in reading and needed a little more one-on-one teaching. The teacher stated that special education would be the best place for me because if I stayed in her class I wouldn't pass. She told my mother and father that I could pass second grade and return with the regular class the next year. I never returned to the regular education class. I was tricked. She tricked me and my parents."
- "My teacher in second grade said that I needed to be in special education. She said the special education teacher would help me get back on track. Once my mom signed the papers and I went to the special education class, the teacher did nothing to help me. If I could talk to the teacher now I would say, 'Why did you trick me? Why did you lie?' My mother would say, 'Why in the hell did you lie to me about my son getting out of special education after one year?' My mother didn't know what special education was."
- "My teacher tricked me. Every day I would go to her class and she would take me to another class. She would leave me there. She said it was for reading help. I found out later that it was special education. I don't even know if anyone signed papers for me to be in special education. My mom didn't!"

It is obvious that many of the participants felt that they were tricked into going into special education. They felt their parents and guardians were misled. Additionally, they felt that the teachers bribed them into staying in special education by giving snacks and allowing students to watch movies every day. As a result, these African American males are now mad, angry, and confused.

"They Don't Care."

All of the participants in this study highlighted the notion that they felt that their teachers and other educational professionals did not care about them. The majority of African American male participants felt as if they were just dumped into special education because many of their regular education teachers did not want to take time with them in the classroom. Note these students' perceptions of their teachers and other educational professionals:

- "The teacher didn't care about me. She just put me in special education because I was learning differently from other students. She didn't take the time to help me understand things. When I asked for help the teacher pretended she didn't hear me. The main reason I fell behind was because she didn't care if I was doing my work or sleeping."

- "One day I was talking to this teacher, this white lady, and she, I think, took something I said the wrong way and when I tried to explain, she just kept getting louder while I tried to talk to her. I didn't [want to] just go crazy so I walked out of the class. She made sure I got expelled and told me I wouldn't be able to find another school. Then I couldn't get into another school for a while. She used me as an example or something. I knew then that she didn't care about me or any of the students."

- "This teacher yelled at me my first day in her class. She told me to sit my ass down. I was mad. I didn't want to stay in her class. She didn't care. All she wanted was for us to sit quietly while she worked on the computer or talked on her cellular phone. My teachers in special education made me feel like, he ain't going to learn, he is stupid. That made me feel like . . . man, like I'm dumb, like I couldn't keep up. All my teachers said they would help me get out of special education but none of them did. Most of my teachers didn't care. They just wanted to get their paycheck."

- "She would put the assignments on the board. She never talked to us until five or ten minutes before the bell. She didn't care what we were doing as long as it looked like we were doing something. She had us do work from the book; as soon as we finished one page she would give us something else until the bell sounded. If your work was wrong, she didn't care. You would get full credit because you were quiet."

Clearly, these comments provide strong evidence from students' perspectives that their experiences were very negative in the special education classroom. As indicated earlier in this study, many of the African American males wanted to learn and have successful careers; however, it appears that their teachers did not care or do anything to help them learn. The majority of these students felt betrayed because the people that were there to help them did not care about their academic well-being.

CONCLUSION

So what can be made of the findings of this particular study? The African American male students interviewed in this study highlighted the major themes when reflecting on their experiences in the special education classroom. First, in the theme "I wanted to be somebody," African American male students clearly expected to succeed in life. Most important, they trusted that their teachers and schools would have prepared them to accomplish their goals. According to Wilson and Corbett (2001), statistics show they will not achieve their educational goals because there are gaps in their education that set the stage for failure.

Another theme from the African American males in this study was "We've been tricked, we've been had, we've been bamboozled." The findings from this theme reveal that the majority of participants felt they and their parents-guardians were tricked into the special education ED placement. Further, the participants stated that teachers allowed them to watch videos, play PlayStation video games, and eat snacks every day. Many of the benefits that these students were given in special education helped to perpetuate the problem. As a result, many of the students fell further and further behind. For example, one student was put in a special education ED class thinking he would be given the opportunity to receive one-on-one help so he could return to his regular class; however, that never happened. As in this example and many others, the African American male students in this study chronicled the many ways they were treated in special education.

The third and final theme in this study is titled, "They Don't Care!" The majority of the participants felt as if their teachers and other educational professionals did not care about their education. Some of the students noted that their teachers didn't care if they slept or smoked in class. Two participants noted that teachers often told them, "You are dumb. You will never make it to middle school, and you're never going to make it to high school." This is a tragedy given that literature reports that students indicate a higher willingness to work and better performance when they feel their teachers care about them (Cushner, McClelland, and Safford, 2006).

Recommendations for Parents and Educators

As a result of this study, the role of the parent in the special education referral process is critical. The following recommendations are essential for parents, school districts, administrators, and teachers:

1. Encourage parents to become actively involved in the special education referral process. This will show educational professionals that you are concerned about the critical stages of the referral process and this will allow parents to understand what services their child should receive if he or she is adequately diagnosed for special education.
2. Recruit a representative to attend the special education referral meetings with you. This will provide you with a representative that has an understanding of special education laws and language.
3. Become involved in your child's education. Oftentimes, education professionals feel that many African American families do not care about their children's education. As a result, make every effort to become involved.

Recommendations for School Districts

School districts play an important part in the educational dilemma of overrepresentation of African American males in special education ED classrooms. The following recommendations are provided to assist school district personnel with this issue:

1. Develop a policy addressing the overrepresentation of African American male students in special education ED programs. Many school districts know they have an overrepresentation of African American males in these special education ED classrooms; however, in many school districts there are currently no plans in place to address this issue.

2. Require professional development workshops and other in-service activities to assist teachers in understanding students from diverse backgrounds. By doing so, educators can understand the cultural capital that students bring to school that can enhance the academic environment.

Recommendations for Administrators

The recommendations below are provided to administrators to assist in reducing the overrepresentation of African American males in special education ED classrooms.

1. Establish a school policy addressing the overrepresentation of African American male students in special education ED classrooms. This will send a strong message that the administration is serious about resolving this issue.
2. Provide support for teachers who are having classroom management issues. Support is critical given that these are the teachers who often refer African American male students to special education.
3. Build relationships with African American male students. Oftentimes, the only time these students see an administrator is when they are in trouble. By building a relationship with these students, they will be able to view their administrators in a different context.

Recommendations for Teachers

Finally, recommendations are provided for teachers because these are the educational professionals who interact with African American males every day in the classroom.

1. Hold African American males to the same standards as their counterparts. Low expectations are the worst form of racism.
2. Be aware of the connection between culture, identity, and learning. Learning should in no way devalue a student's background.
3. Collaborative relationships with parents should be forged with a renewed energy. Oftentimes, many teachers do not think parents

want to be involved; however, many times parents are not involved because they are not invited to participate.

REFERENCES

Artiles, A., and Trent, S. (1994). Overrepresentation of minority students in special education: A continuing debate. *Journal of Special Education* 27, 410–37.
Brown, D. (2001). The examination of the overrepresentation of African
American students in special education programs from a sociocultural per-
spective. Unpublished doctoral dissertation, University of Virginia, Char-
lottesville.
Chinn, P., and Hughes, S. (1987). Representation of minority students in spe-
cial education class. *Remedial and Special Education* 8(4), 41–46.
Coutinho, M., and Oswald, D. (1998). Ethnicity and special education research:
Identifying questions and methods. *Behavioral Disorders* 24, 66–73.
Cushner, K., McClelland, A., and Safford, P. (2006). *Human diversity in edu-
cation: an integrative approach.* Boston: McGraw-Hill Co.
Dunn, L. (1968). Special education for the mildly retarded: Is much of it jus-
tifiable? *Exceptional Children* 23, 5–21.
Gibbs, J. T. (1988). *Young, black and male in America: An endangered
species.* Dover, MA: Auburn House.
Glaser, B. (1992). *Doing grounded theory: Issues and discussion.* Mill Valley,
CA: Sociology Press.
Goffman, E. (1963). *Stigma: Notes on the management of spoiled identity.* En-
glewood Cliffs, NJ: Prentice Hall.
Grant, P. (1992). Using special education to destroy black boys. *The Negro Ed-
ucational Review* 63, 17–21.
Harry, B. (1992). Restructuring the participation of African American families
in special education. *Exceptional Children* 59, 123–31.
Harry, B., and Anderson, M. (1994). The disproportionate placement of
African American males in special education programs: A critique of the
process. *Journal of Negro Education* 63, 602–19.
Heller, K. (1992). Placing children in special education: Equity through valid
educational practices. *Final Report* 24, 21–22.
Hilliard, A. G. (1992). The meaning of KMT (Ancient Egyptian) history for
contemporary African American experience. *Phylon* 49, 10–22.
Hilliard, A. (1990). Misunderstanding and testing intelligence. In J. I. Good-
lad and P. Keating (Eds.), *Access to knowledge: An agenda for our nation's
schools* (pp. 145–57). New York: College Board.

Individuals with Disability Education Act Amendment of 1997, P.L. No. 105–17. U.S. Department of Education, Washington, DC: Author.

Irvine, J. J. (1990). *Black students and school: Politics, practices and prescriptions*. Westport, CT: Greenwood Press.

Irvine, J. J., and York, D. E. (1993). Teacher perceptions: Why do African-American, Hispanic, and Vietnamese students fail? In S. W. Rothstein (Ed.), *Handbook of Schools in Urban America* (pp. 161–73). Westport, CT: Greenwood Press.

Kunjufu, J. (2002). *Black students. Middle class teachers*. Chicago: African American Images.

Kunjufu, J. (2005). *Keeping black boys out of special education*. Chicago: African American Images.

Larson, S. (1975). The influence of teacher expectation on the school performance of handicapped children. *Focus on Exceptional Children* 6, 1–14.

Lincoln, Y., and Guba, E. (1985). *Naturalistic inquiry*. Beverly Hills: Sage.

Markowitz, J., Garcia, S., and Eichelberger, J. H. (1997). *Addressing the disproportionate placement of students from racial and ethnic minority groups in special education programs and classes*. Alexandria, VA: National Association of State Directors of Special Education.

Miles, M., and Huberman, A. (1994). *Qualitative data analysis*. Thousand Oaks, CA: Sage.

Mincy, R. B. (1994). *Nurturing young black males: Challenges to agencies, programs, and social policy*. Washington, DC: Urban Institute Press.

Oswald, D. P., Coutinho, M. J., Best, A. M., and Singh, N. N. (1999). Ethnic representation in special education: The influence of school-related economic and demographic variables. *Journal of Special Education* 21, 155–80.

Parrish, T. (2002). *Racial disparities in the identification, funding and provision of special education*. Cambridge, MA: Harvard Education Press.

Patton, J. M. (1998). The disproportionate representation of African Americans in special education: Looking behind the curtain for understanding and solutions. *The Journal of Special Education* 32, 1.

Reiff, H., Gerber, P., and Ginsburg, R. (1997). *Exceeding expectations: Successful adults with learning disability*. Austin, TX: Pro-Ed.

Reschly, D. (1996). *Disproportionate minority representation in general and special education programs: Patterns, issues, and alternatives*. Des Moines, IA: Drake University, Resource Center/MPRRC.

Serwatka, T., Deering, S., and Grant, P. (1995). Disproportionate representation of African Americans in emotionally handicapped classes. *Journal of Black Studies* 25, 492–506.

United States Department of Education. (1997). *Nineteenth annual report to Congress to assure the free appropriate public education of all children with disabilities.*

United States Justice Department. (1997). *Crime in the United States*: A*nnual publication in which the FBI compiles volume and rate of crime offenses for the nation, the states, and individual agencies.*

Watkins, M., and Kurtz, D. (2001). Using solution-focused intervention to address African American male overrepresentation in special education: A case study. *Children & Schools* 23, 223–34.

Willie, C., Garibaldi, A., and Reed, W. (1991). *The education of African Americans.* Boston: William Monroe Trotter Institute.

Wilson, B., and Corbett. D. (2001) *Listening to urban kids: School reform and the teachers they want.* New York: SUNY Press.

CHAPTER 9

The Challenge of Implementing Black History

Student Narratives of a Black History Program

ABUL PITRE, RUTH RAY, AND LURIA STUBBLEFIELD

INTRODUCTION

Public school systems throughout America have been faced with the problem of implementing curricula that reflect a pluralistic society—in particular, curricula regarding the African American experience (Banks, 2008; Wilhelm, 1994). This problem has often led to student protests demanding the implementation of courses that reflect a more diverse society (Rhoads, 1998; "Proposal to Scuttle Afrocentric Curricula," 1997). Administrators and teachers have hypothesized of ways to promote a more multicultural-centered curriculum; however, in many school systems the idea of a multicultural curriculum has not yet become a reality.

One of the major problems around the implementation of black history in some public schools is the fear that it will explode the official story. Pinar describes the official story as the story we like to tell ourselves regarding American freedom, justice, and equality. Historically, some groups were deprived of these freedoms through laws that declared them second-class citizens. African Americans in their sojourn in North America have been denied knowledge of self. Thus, the historical issues around black history and its relevance are alive and well in contemporary times.

Some have argued that there is no need for black history because it is divisive. Others have argued that black history will result in the self-ghettozation of African American students. The debate regarding black history is ongoing. Recently schools in Wisconsin, California, and Louisiana have witnessed student protests as a result of black history activities. In Milwaukee, a school board member's effort to remove

Afro-centric curricula from the schools resulted in an emotional protest by hundreds of parents and raised questions about what is being taught in multicultural programs ("Proposal to Scuttle Afrocentric Curricula," 1997). In Los Angeles two racial flare-ups demonstrated the challenges faced by many school districts. In February 1999, a white principal at a mostly Hispanic elementary school was beaten up outside of the school by two men who told him, "We don't want you here anymore, Principal" (Covarrubias, 1999). In another incident, Inglewood High School dropped both Black History Month and Cinco de Mayo for fear of the violence and student walkouts that had occurred in the past. Adding to the problem at Inglewood even after dropping these programs, the school was forced to close for one day in May because of a riot that required dozens of police to be called (Covarrubias, 1999).

A similar protest took place in a Louisiana school and made the headlines for several weeks, with the controversy lasting well over one year. The controversy began when a few white teachers walked out of a black history program, prompting black students, parents, and teachers to become upset. Immediately following the program, a white teacher phoned the school board to inform them that there would be trouble at the school as a result. The next day the school was surrounded with school board personnel, sheriff's deputies, and newspaper reporters. The headline of the newspaper declared, "A Contingent of School Board administrators and a Cadre of Deputies, including the chief deputy with the Sheriff's Office were patrolling the halls" ("Controversy at High School," 1994).

The black students complained that during the Black History Month program a year earlier, all of the white students checked out of school just before the speaker had arrived ("Controversy at High School," 1994). One month after the 1994 black history program, one of the teachers who walked out of the program had a confrontation with a student. The local newspaper printed on its front page "Teacher Attacked by Student." In the article the teacher claimed that ever since the speech given during the program, he had felt animosity from black parents and students at the school ("Teacher Attacked by Student," 1994). As a result of these events, black parents demanded that the teachers who walked out of the program be removed from the school. A parent leader of a newly formed organization called Concerned Parents stated, "We are asking the two teachers to resign because they are racist. It has happened before and it just got bad after the Black History program" ("School troubles," 1994).

The president of the local National Association for the Advancement of Colored People (NAACP) expressed his feelings about the situation by saying, "The system is racist for allowing those types of things to happen . . . We met with the superintendent last year about White teachers leading White students out of those programs." He also stated that the school board had been approached about implementing a policy that would deter this type of behavior: "We approached the superintendent a week prior to the assembly and asked that a policy be established" ("School Troubles," 1994).

Other problems with the implementation of black history curricula can be seen in studies conducted by Alexander (1982) and Wilhelm (1994). In a study of thirty-six elementary public school principals in Chesapeake and Maryland public school systems, Alexander reported that the designation of February as Black History Month had "negligible impact on actual observances in the schools" (1982). In Wilhelm's 1994 study, which surveyed forty-eight elementary schools in the Dallas-Fort Worth, Texas, area, he reported that many of the schools had no policy regarding the implementation of Black History Month. Wilhelm stated, "The large percentage of schools with no planned observances suggested that this kind of *laissez-faire* policy may be common place in most districts" (1994, p. 220).

The finding that most school districts have no policy with regard to Black History Month is consistent with Alexander's findings: "No signs of leadership were offered at the central administration level to actually provide programmatic leadership [regarding Black History Month] to the schools" (1982, p. 6). As Wilhelm (1994) describes it, "Most public school curricula related to Black History and culture is antiseptic and lacking in analysis of the Black experience in a meaningful and real life manner" (p. 217). While administrators and teachers are cognizant of this problem, solutions have been slow in coming. This article explores student leaders' experiences regarding the controversy and student protest surrounding a black history program at their school.

THE CHALLENGE

The challenge of implementing a multicultural curriculum is one that is not going away. Today the current curriculum is being challenged to become more multicultural (Banks, 2008). Challenges are being put

forward by African Americans, Asian Americans, and Latinos "for inclusion and reformulation of the canon used to select content for the
school, college, and university curriculum" (Banks, 2008, p. 25). Furthermore, coalitions are being formed with white students who wish to
see a more inclusive curriculum (Banks, 2008).

Issues around the implementation of black history and multicultural
curricula have caused a new student movement that is the primary
cause of student activism in the 1990s (Rhoads, 1998). Rhoads has
"found multiculturalism to be the number one cause of student unrest
in the 1990s" (1998, p. 24). Added to this fact is that it is projected that
by the year 2020 students of color will make up 46 percent of the nation's school-aged youth (Pallas, Natriello, and McDill, 1989).

Under the umbrella of multicultural education curriculum reform is
the push for black history, which is sometimes synonymously used with
Afro-centric history (Banks, 2008). African American students, parents, and community groups are leading the push for a curriculum that
reflects the experience of Africans and African Americans (Chemelynski, 1990; Lee, 1992). This challenge, according to Banks (2008), "will
continue, will be fierce and will at times become ugly and pernicious.
It will take diverse forms, expressions and shapes" (p. 27).

In order to meet the challenge associated with issues around the implementation of black history and critical multicultural education, it is
important to study controversies and protest with regard to the implementation of black history. More important is the need for studies to ascertain what the experience is like for students involved with this issue.
This could go a long way in helping those for and against the implementation of black history to reach some common ground. A major
problem with the implementation of black history lies in the lack of
studies about the experiences of proponents and opponents of this issue.

PURPOSE OF THE STUDY

The purpose of this study was to examine the experiences of the student leaders in order to ascertain how their experiences of the black history program and student protest were viewed at the time of the controversy and the effect of this phenomenon on their personal lives.
Findings from this study could enhance the knowledge base of school

districts and administrators planning to incorporate black history programs into the curriculum. Furthermore, these experiences may provide an additional opportunity for school administrators to look at the impact of black history on the attitudes of students. In addition, findings from this study could encourage teachers and administrators to reflect on issues of justice and equity.

RESEARCH QUESTIONS

The research on student activism suggested the need for a phenomenological study to examine the narrative experience of student leaders. We modified Seidman's (1998) in-depth phenomenological interviewing approach to ascertain the narrative experience of student leaders. This approach has three levels of questioning: (1) Gathering background information about the participants; (2) Investigating how individuals recall events associated with the phenomenon in relation to their personal thoughts and actions; and (3) Exploring the meaning and impact of the phenomenon on the participants. For the purpose of this chapter, two major questions are highlighted:

1. Did this black history program impact African American student leaders' perspectives on school and the larger society?
2. How did African American student leaders perceive the attitudes of those white teachers and students who walked out of the black history program?

DISCUSSION AND FINDINGS

Critical pedagogy in examining power relationships and how they intersect with education can be used to examine the issues around the controversial black history program in this study. One of the questions that critical pedagogy seeks to examine is, "Whose knowledge and for what purpose?" Historically, the education of African Americans has been designed by what Watkins calls "the White architects of Black education" for the purpose of control. Watkins (2001) notes the following about education: "Organized education, much like religion, has been long influenced by the forces of the power structure, the state and those with an ideological agenda" (p. 10). Woodson makes a similar observation when he points out that "the education of the Negroes, then, the most important thing in the uplift of Negroes, is almost entirely in the hands of those who enslaved them and now segregate them" (1999, p. 22).

These points are significant as the majority of African Americans even in contemporary times do not have the power to determine what they believe their children should know. The issue of white control over African American education was clearly demonstrated in the controversy around this black history program. Despite the positive impact that this black history program and African American studies course had on African American students, the program was viewed with resentment by some white teachers. Some white teachers felt threatened by the awakened consciousness of African American students regarding the prevalent racism in school and the larger society. The invited speaker pointed out the power relationships that existed in the larger society and how this impacted African American people. Ultimately what the speaker had done was create a dialectical dialogue with the students. McLaren (2007) summarizes what happened at this black history program when he says, "The purpose of dialectal educational theory, then, is to provide students with a model that permits them to examine the underlying political, social, and economic foundations of the larger White supremacist capitalist society" (p. 195). This dialectical discourse with students resulted in an unveiling of racism both in school and the larger society. In addition, the speaker raised the consciousness of students so that they could locate themselves.

The student leaders in this study discussed how this black history program made them more aware of the racial inequities that are displayed in both the school and larger society. One of the important goals of multicultural education, according to Banks (2008), is to help students to work from the social-action approach. The social-action approach allows individuals and groups to take action on important social issues. As a result of this eye-opening experience, students were able to work from Banks' social-action approach. Student leaders expressed that as a result of these experiences they became more aware to the racial inequalities that exist. Student leaders reported the following regarding their new consciousness:

- Well, the program and all that we have been through, it gave me an awareness, to not be so passive and sit back. And accept what people do to you or say to you. You know, you can always go out and read it for yourself and find out more. It has just made me a stronger person, you know, to deal with things that happened in my life. Now, I could look back at those times and pull something positive from that. You know, it made my will stronger, my determination. I know we may have failed in our efforts to get him [the reassigned teacher] back at our school, that didn't take away anything, from what we gained from the experience.

- I think I would be kind of narrow-minded. I probably wouldn't understand things about whites and blacks. Because I would be blind to a lot of the facts that I was taught by my teacher. And you know, when certain things that happen to me, you know, the few encounters that I had with white people, I probably would have brushed it off and probably would have thought it is something that just happens. Because, you know, nobody made an issue of it. I guess they were trying to hide us from all the facts that made us understand who we are and why things happen around us.

- What made it different was the speaker that we had for this particular program emphasized us as a black people and the situation that we are in and we need to stand together. To overcome the obstacles that we were placed in—and it wasn't by choice that we were in the United States. And we were struggling because of this and because of that, and it wasn't our fault, but that we can't just say it's not our fault. We have to stand together and to do something about it. But speakers at the past black history program just mainly emphasized [how important it is] to get an education. And they talked about the black leaders from the past that stood up for civil rights, but they didn't actually explain that they had to go through this or had to go through that, in order to struggle to get it. They just said, "Okay, yes, they were good people and they helped us out." That was it.

- I know how to ask a whole bunch of questions when I need to because in the past I used to just keep my mouth shut and just let certain people just run over me. And now today people look at me like, "Let her do her thing, she knows what she is doing, she is well prepared." And the time before this experience, I used to be just hush and not look for certain things.

- It made me realize a lot. It made me more open to listening to people and how they feel about Black History. A lot of the issues with the school are political. There is a lot of prejudice and when you see it, and it is actually right up in your face, it is different.

- Well, this program was different from the traditional Black History programs. You didn't get the regular traditional talk about Martin Luther King. The speaker talked about things that were going on in the United States, how black people were—he was teaching us knowledge about ourselves, about what was going on around us. [He told us that] we should open up our eyes and see what was going on and that was something different from traditional Black History programs.

- It made me look at myself and how I treat others. And how others treat me. Whether or not I'm being treated equal. I grew a lot after the program; it opened my eyes a lot.

Campbell (2004) notes that consciousness gives one awareness of oneself and the environment. In analyzing their environment, students were able to locate the source of their oppression. Macedo (2000) brilliantly illustrates this point when he comments on Freire's work, *Pedagogy of the Oppressed*: "Imagine that instead of writing *Pedagogy of the Oppressed* Freire had written *Pedagogy of the Disenfranchised*. The first title utilizes discourse that names the oppressor, whereas the second fails to do so. If you have an 'oppressed,' you must have an 'oppressor.' *Pedagogy of the Disenfranchised* dislodges the agent of the action while leaving doubt who bears the responsibility for such action" (p. 21). The alternate term leaves the ground wide open for blaming the victim of disenfranchisement for his or her own predicament. As a result of this new consciousness, some white teachers feared that their attitudes, dispositions, and the role of white supremacy had been unveiled, thus causing them to seek some form of retribution on the students, the teacher who organized the black history program, and the principal. Some white teachers, administrators, and students also saw this as a threat to their dominant positions in the school.

A deeper analysis of the situation at this high school reveals that part of the problem was a direct result of the monocultural attitudes and white privilege that existed prior to the black history program. Previously, white teachers, administrators, and students walked out of black history programs or either checked out of school without any reprimand from those in authority. These monocultural attitudes represent the *luxury of ignorance* characterized by what Gary Howard (2006) describes in his book, *We Can't Teach What We Don't Know*. The white teachers at this school seem to have been isolated from the history of oppressed groups in America. Thus, they were entrapped by the luxury of ignorance. Howard notes:

> I realize that members of the dominant group in any society do not necessarily have to know anything about those people who are not like them. For our survival and the carrying on of the day to day activities of our lives, most White Americans do not have to engage in any meaningful personal connection with people who are different. This is not a luxury available to people who live outside of dominance and must, for their survival, understand the essential social nuances of those in power. The luxury of ignorance reinforces and perpetuates White isolation. (p. 12)

Student leaders voiced their concerns about the disrespect white teachers displayed toward the study of black history:

- We figured teachers are role models and you don't just get up and walk out of a black history program. I mean, normally in a black history program, you could hear talking. The students were laughing and talking and you know, nobody was paying attention. But I mean in this program people were really listening to what this man had to say. And for them [white teachers] to get up and walk out was disrespect.
- I think the black students felt like they were being disrespected because the white teachers walked out and the white teachers walked out because they felt that what the speaker was saying wasn't positive. When actually it was the truth and we felt like, "If it is the truth, why should we be kept from the truth?" You know, and we're not like the white students; they have everything they need, they are not socially challenged, or economically challenged, they

have a much better percentage rate of people going to college and people succeeding. You know, we felt like, "If this is just our month or our day to hear something positive, to do us some good, why should they be upset about it?"

- When a lot of white people walked out of our black history program and we believed that if we sat and learned, it was true, teachers walked out first and some students followed. And we just felt that this wasn't right; we sit and learn white history in class and we don't walk out. We were learning something and we felt it was disrespect for them to walk out on our black history program.
- It was very stressful, especially how the minority group [white teachers and students] handled the things. They weren't forced to attend the black history program and the white parents didn't want their children to interact with the program. For them not to be there was disrespectful. It is a part of history and just the title "Black History" doesn't mean anything. It is actually a part of history. We did sit in class and learn about Abe Lincoln and Theodore Roosevelt and everybody else. But very seldom [do] we learn about our heritage.

The students' comments are reflective of McIntosh's *white privilege* phenomena, clearly demonstrating that the white teachers could do as they pleased without fear of being reprimanded because of their relationship with those in power, which was based on their race. In addition, black history programs in the past had been largely presented from the perspective of the dominant group.

Previous black history programs offered what Banks calls the *contribution approach*. The contribution approach simply celebrates and glorifies the accomplishments of token African Americans. Nieto references this approach when she points out how Dr. Martin Luther King Jr. has been historically engineered to fit the ideology of those in power. For example, it is okay to mention Dr. King's dream, but never his opposition to the Vietnam War (Nieto and Bode, 2008) or his meeting with Elijah Muhammad. In this sense, the black history programs of the past served the interest of those in the dominant group who wished to remain veiled so as not to display their complicit racist attitudes.

Finally, Kincheloe and Steinberg (1997) note that critical pedagogy and Afro-centrism merge together for social and curricular change. A critical pedagogical approach to presenting black history can empower and raise the consciousness of students. The use of critical pedagogy is a very straightforward approach that does not attempt to sugarcoat the realities of the African American experience. More important, critical pedagogy helps to reveal the role of power relations and how those relations can be uprooted. Freire (2000) notes that it is only when the oppressed come to the realization that the oppressor mentality has been internalized into their consciousness that the road to liberation can begin. In this study, the Louisiana high school's black history program raised the consciousness of students, which "led these formerly passive students to turn against their domestication and the attempt to domesticate reality" (p. 75). The students in this study demonstrate the power of reflection and action, a praxis that can lead to a more humanizing society.

CONCLUSION

This study revealed that there were three major reasons for the monocultural attitudes that pervaded this southern school: (1) The school held inadequate policies regarding black history programs, (2) Some teachers and administrators had insufficient knowledge of multicultural education, and (3) There was a lack of respect for black history by some white teachers.

If schools are to achieve equity and justice, teachers and other school personnel must be cognizant of their beliefs and practices that may alienate students who do not come from the dominant culture. Student leaders reported a new awareness as a result of this black history program. They saw this experience as something that made them more aware of the persistent racism that produces inequality in school and in the larger society. This new consciousness thus paved the way for them to become empowered.

The growing diversity in American schools demands more than just an addition of various ethnic groups into the curriculum; it also requires serious truth telling. This truth telling must be grounded in issues of justice and equity. At the core of educating for diversity is black history.

The current multicultural education movement grew out of the African American struggle for equity and justice in American society. It is unfortunate that the teachers in this study displayed negative attitudes toward black history. It is hoped that teachers who oppose diversity should observe that there is unity in diversity, which is demonstrated when observing flowers in a garden. All of the flowers grow in a common soil and each needs water for survival. In the same way we all seek freedom, justice, and equality. As demonstrated in this article, it is difficult to predict when or even if the controversy surrounding black history will end; however, it is important to understand that educators, parents, and students all play a vital role in ensuring that the mis-education ends.

REFERENCES

Alexander, C. (1982). The frequency and types of African American history month celebration programs in the Chesapeake school system between 1980–1982. ECA Associates, Chesapeake, VA. (ERIC Document Reproduction Service No. 220355).

Banks, J. (2008). *An introduction to multicultural education* (4th ed.). Boston: Allyn & Bacon.

Campbell, D. (2004). *Choosing democracy: A practical guide to multicultural education* (4th ed.). Boston: Allyn & Bacon.

Chemelynski, C. (1990). Controversy attends schools with all-black, all male classes. *The Executive Director* 12, 16–18.

Controversy at high school. (1994, February 27). *Opelousas Daily World.*

Covarrubias, A. (1999, February). LA schools battle racial upheavals. *The Bakersfield Californian.*

Freire, P. (2000). *Pedagogy of the oppressed.* New York: Continuum.

Howard, G. (2006). *We can't teach what we don't know: White teachers in multiracial schools.* New York: Teachers College Press.

Kincheloe, J., and Steinberg, S. (1997). *Changing multiculturalism.* Buckingham, PA: Open University Press.

Lee, C. D. (1992). Profile of an independent black institution: African centered education at work. *Journal of Negro Education* 61(2), 160–77.

Macedo, D. (2000). Introduction. In P. Freire, *Pedagogy of the oppressed* (30th Anniversary ed., pp. 11–28). New York: Continuum.

McLaren, P. (2007). *Life in urban schools: An introduction to critical pedagogy in the foundations of education* (4th ed.). Boston: Allyn & Bacon.

Nieto, S., and Bode, P. (2008). *Affirming diversity: The socio-political context of multicultural education* (4th ed.). New York: Longman.

Pallas, A. M., Natriello, G., and McDill, E. L. (1989). The changing nature of the disadvantaged population: Current dimensions and future trends. *Educational Researcher 18,* 16–22.

Proposal to scuttle Afrocentric curricula sparks protest (1997, January 15). *Education Week.*

Rhoads, R. (1998). *Student activism in an age of cultural diversity.* Baltimore: Johns Hopkins University Press.

School troubles: Parents want to oust principal, 2 teachers. (1994, March 31) *Opelousas Daily World.*

Seidman, I. (1998). *Interviewing as qualitative research: A guide for researcher in education and social services.* New York: Teachers College Press.

Teacher attacked by student. (1994, March 22). *Opelousas Daily World.*

Watkins, W. (2001). The *white architects of black education: Ideology and power in America 1865–1954.* New York: Teachers College Press.

Wilhelm, R. (1994). Exploring the practice of rhetoric gap: Current curriculum for African American history month in some Texas elementary schools. *Journal of Curriculum and Instruction 9,* 217–33.

Woodson, C. G. (1999). *The mis-education of the Negro* (11th ed.). Trenton, NJ: First Africa World Press.

CHAPTER 10

The Conspicuously Unnoticed

High-Achieving, African American Mathematics Students in Schools Deemed Academically Unacceptable

PETER SHEPPARD

INTRODUCTION

Over a century ago there existed considerable disparities in nearly every aspect of education from achievement to facilities. Similarly, the current profile of educational opportunity for a significant segment of African American children mirrors that of the early twentieth century; predominantly African American schools are most often housed in crumbling facilities, suffer from starved budgets, and lack essential resources (Sullivan, 2004). The No Child Left Behind Act (NCLB), touted as an equalizer of educational opportunity, further contributed to this dark period of education for minorities through its accountability mandates (Kohn, 2000). Repercussions from accountability systems are largely based on test scores, and prior research can attest (namely Horn, 2003) African Americans have been greatly underrepresented among the highest scorers on standardized tests. Consequently, African Americans and schools with high concentrations of African Americans are most likely to be perniciously "burnt at the high stakes" (Kohn, 2000).

Often unnoticed in the plethora of negative research findings are those students who excel in schools that some consider deplorable; therefore, the objectives of this study were to determine (1) the reasons why high-achieving mathematics students have been able to thrive in schools labeled *academically unacceptable* and (2) why they have chosen to stay in these *academically unacceptable* schools despite having the option to leave for a better performing school.

W. E. B. Du Bois proposed that academically elite students be central figures in overcoming academic and social obstacles. He referred to this group as the *Talented Tenth*. Du Bois (1903) stated: "The *Talented Tenth* must be made leaders of thought and missionaries of culture among their people. No others can do this work . . . [This society] is going to be saved by its exceptional men." Du Bois' conjecture provides a noteworthy justification for this study, which focuses on high-achieving mathematics students who are conceivably among today's Talented Tenth and are thus likely to contribute to solving enigmas associated with African American students' deficiencies in mathematics.

RELATED LITERATURE

Milner (2002) indicated that African American high-achieving students face several challenges, including underfunded schools with meager resources, emotional and psychological distress (from peers and societal perceptions), exclusion and isolation, and powerlessness. Furthermore, those African American high achievers from low-income families must also endure the cumulative effects of exposure to community violence, poverty, racism, oppression, and other forms of abuse (Jipguep and Sanders-Phillips, 2003). Ladson-Billings (1998) pointed out that students of color are often misrepresented as "dangerous minds" that live and learn in "dangerous times."

Despite the presence of ominous circumstances, there are some students who find ways to rise above the aforementioned adversities. Maton, Hrabowski, and Grief (1998) found that high levels of parental academic engagement, strictness, nurturance, and community connectedness collectively appeared to counteract the negative contextual influences of neighborhood, peers, schools, and society. Martin (2000) had similar findings, pointing out that family and teacher support, individual goals, and the need to help others through community service were all contributors to the mathematics success of African American students. Tucker, Herman, Pederson, Vogel, and Reinke (2000) found that African American students believe keys to their academic success include (1) academic preparation, (2) positive peer influences in promoting academic success, and (3) praise and encouragement by teachers and parents.

The above research has addressed the question of how African American high-achieving students circumvent problems in their schools, but the emergence of accountability systems provides a strong incentive to revisit the issue. Specifically, this study is distinguishable from past studies because it is placed in the context of state-designated *academically unacceptable* schools, which means African American students in this study were faced with the additional burden of attending a publicly bemoaned school. The current research literature is deficient in addressing this issue; therefore, it is the aim of this study to add scholarship to this topic.

MODES OF INQUIRY

Research studies by Maton, Hrabowski, and Grief (1998), Martin (2000), and Tucker and colleagues (2000) provide a blueprint for how to approach this study methodologically. Similar to the previously mentioned research, this study sought to gain a descriptive understanding of the participants' experiences. Thus, a qualitative approach was appropriate.

Two Louisiana public schools were selected for this study: Lake High School and River High School (pseudonyms). The Louisiana Department of Education labeled these schools *academically unacceptable* based on the schools' academic performances on criterion-referenced tests (60 percent), norm-referenced tests (30 percent), attendance (5 percent), and dropout rate (5 percent). In fall 2004, 75 schools were labeled *academically unacceptable*. Lake High and River High were among the few high schools to enroll at least five successful African American mathematics students. For the sake of this study, high-achieving students were defined as those students who scored at the advanced or mastery levels in mathematics on Louisiana's Graduate Exit Exam (GEE) required for high school graduation. The author realizes said definition has limits, but in the era of high-stakes testing, high scores on standardized tests are considered the apex of achievement, and students immediately earn the favor of school districts and state educational agencies. In spring 2003, only 6 percent of African Americans scored at the advanced or mastery levels in mathematics on the GEE, while nearly 49 percent of African

Americans failed the mathematics section (Louisiana Department of Education, 2003).

Moreover, the above high schools were even more ideal for this study because they were lauded for exemplifying significant academic improvement even though both schools were considered academically unacceptable. The state recognized both schools for their efforts to improve by bestowing upon them the "Recognized Academic Growth" label. Finally, the results presented here are modified and will include narratives from eleven students (seven males, four females) participating in the study.

DATA SOURCES OR EVIDENCE

Each of the 11 students in the study completed a 10-item, open-ended survey related to the research questions. The students then participated in one-hour taped small-group-interview sessions as a follow-up to the survey results. In all of the above situations, the group interviews took place within a week of the participants completing the open-ended survey.

Results from the interviews were presented in a format similar to what Merriam (1998) describes as a narrative analysis because first-person accounts are given. These interviews also share the characteristics of what Seidman (1998) labels a profile of participants. In both the profile and narrative analysis, the reader is allowed his own interpretation, whether contrary to or in confirmation of the researcher's conclusions. Additionally, all data from interviews and responses from questionnaires given to students were coded and analyzed for congruent themes.

RESULTS

One of the aims of this study was to highlight the often overlooked resilience of high-achieving mathematics students in academically unacceptable schools (Martin, 2000). The results presented will provide the reader with a few exemplars of successful students in academically unacceptable schools and it is hoped that these results will provide greater understanding of the issues discussed in this study. Further, although this study only provided descriptions of students from two low-performing schools, it reflects larger issues associated with low-performing schools, high-achieving mathematics students, and school choice. In the aggregate, the above issues in fact represent the building of theory related to "unacceptable" low-performing schools and African American high achievers.

Research Question #1

The first major research question in this study sought to *determine the reasons why successful mathematics students have been able to thrive in academically unacceptable schools.*

Student participants in this study primarily attributed their success to their mathematics teachers and their own personal character traits. The participants mentioned that teachers' ability to separate mathematics into comprehensible chunks ultimately allowed them to flourish in mathematics. This approach to teaching led to an increase in student confidence in mathematics, an apparent decrease in mathematics anxiety, and an overall change in attitude toward school among student participants (as mentioned by student participants). The second most prevalent reason the participants felt they were successful was because of personal traits they possessed. The participants identified a range of personal traits that included the ability to focus, desire to succeed, determination, and curious-inquisitive nature. Collectively, it was also evident that these students had a strong belief in self. Each of the students circuitously or directly pointed out that believing they could succeed contributed to their success in mathematics. Bauman (1998) points out that African Americans who take a role in their own advancement invest more time in their education and thus seek greater economic opportunities as a result of their personal commitment to education. The following students' comments support this theory:

> The fact that I am considered a successful mathematics student has a lot to do with my math teacher, Mr. Greece, because math was my worst subject. There were times when I would want to just give up, [thinking] maybe it's just not for me, but he told me "'Don't give up, it's not hard, you can do it.'" From there it was all me. I began studying harder. I began to get on

top of everything. When I am determined to do something, I will do it and I was determined to succeed in math. I became even more serious about my work once I tasted success. Plus, I am motivated to graduate. It's like my biggest thing that I have is that I want to graduate. That's my real motivation: graduation. —*Sara*, River High School

I have to give credit to my mathematics teachers because I believe that I am a success because of their teaching. In addition I have been a successful mathematics student and will continue to be successful because I do not just rely on the education I get at this school. I read books beyond the school walls. I have a great interest in doing that. I guess it is my inquisitive temperament. I guess it is the way my parents raised me and what I learned kind of through life. So if you want to be successful don't rely solely on the school. School is only a portion of what is required to be a success. I encourage [those who want to succeed] to read books, watch educational programs, and use the *Google* search engine. I think that kind of reflects my view of education. —*Zeke*, Lake High School

The reason why I am a strong student in math is because the teachers that I had taught me well. I listened and paid attention in class because I did not think I was that good in math at one time. So I started attending school tutorial programs after school, on Saturdays, and during the summer. All of the teachers in the programs helped me be successful. Once I started doing well, all of them became very supportive of my success. They often complimented me on doing well. It could be because they really took time with me. Anything I didn't understand they always explained it to me, step by step. They kept going over it with me. Anything that could have helped me improve, they offered it to me. So I think they wanted the best for me. —*Pandora*, River High School

I think we have some good teachers here. I take advantage of that. Some kids do not. Like when I had Ms. Leavy, I would stop the class and make them be quiet. Ms. Leavy used to talk to me about how I was doing in class, so then I started paying attention and participating in class. She tried to make it fun for me and I started catching on a little at a time. Basically, that's why I have a lot of respect for her. She doesn't teach here anymore, but every time I see her I always speak to her and tell her how good she made me. Without her, I would probably have dropped out. Now math is my favorite subject. I'm successful because I had people like Ms. Leavy who were forcing me to learn. That made me want to learn and I want to do well in my classes. I reached a point when I felt I was ready to learn different things and that turned into success. —*Titus*, River High School

One student participant had a peculiar set of circumstances. He explained that he had poor mathematics teachers in the past and a tumultuous, dismal home life. He attributes his success to a determination to be the best he can be and to "be better than my family." His case is even more intriguing because it implies that his personal tenacity and self-confidence offset the oppressive state of affairs in his home and school life.

The thing that made me successful is that I have never shied away from being focused on my education. I don't think it really had anything to do with the teachers. I had two mathematics teachers last year and both of them were not that good. If I would have had a good teacher like Mr. Egypt, who teaches me this year, I would have had an even better score on the GEE.

My success also comes from me wanting to prove people wrong because when I get home I get called "stupid." I tell them, "I am not stupid and I am going to be better than you." Well, it really makes me want to try harder because I know I am going to be better than them and that's going to be the final word on it. So, I have to do well because my home is so horrible. I really want to do something better with my life. —*Vernon*, Lake High School

Although parents and early-school backgrounds were mentioned by the student participants as factors in success, those responses were not pervasive. Three of the students answered that their parents were, indeed, contributors to their success. They identified parental discipline, encouragement, and general rearing as the main things parents had done to ensure their academic development. This, however, was not a major thread in the interviews.

One of the keys to my success is that I am curious. "Curiosity killed the cat," but in my case, curiosity made the cat a genius. Like if I do not know something and I am curious about it, I am going to look it up. I think my curiosity started out when I was a kid. I used to play with Lego toys and wonder how different pieces can fit together and make something bigger.

You start toying with that and everything else starts to get bigger and better. I have to admit my family does contribute a lot to my success. My dad is a police officer, so I have a certain respect for authority. You sort of listen to what they have to say in different ways and it has that influence. My mom raised me in church school for most of my elementary school years and then she put me in home school for seventh and eighth grade. Since my brother got into trouble when he was my age, they needed to show me what not to do. They talked to me about stuff. They rode me. They said, "Don't do this and you know what's going to happen if you do this." They make sure I'm using common sense. — *Yann*, Lake High School

My parents have a big influence on me. My mom likes to brag to her friends and family about how well I'm doing. That inspires me to try harder. She also expects a lot from me. If I make all As and one B, she will say, "Why did you make the B?" She says As are what I am supposed to make. When I do well I think I am doing it for both my parents. For me, I like doing well in math because it's my favorite subject. — *Ulysses*, Lake High School

Research Question #2

The second major research question in this study asks, *Why have successful mathematics students chosen to stay in academically unacceptable schools despite having the option to leave for a better performing school?*

All of the student participants in this study firmly believed that remaining at their present school was the best choice for them. The reasons cited all revolved around their strong identification with their schools. Students' familiarity with school rules, friends, teachers, and atmospheres in general convinced them to continue attending the academically unacceptable schools. Some even mentioned that their schools had developed family atmospheres. They believed that a change would not be worth building a new school culture or cultivating new relationships with teachers and students. Similarly, prior research has indicated that students who identify with the academic culture of a school are more motivated to achieve and experience higher educational gains than their peers who do not (Finn, 1989; Finn and

Cox, 1992). Further, as evinced by student responses, these students trusted their respective schools. Goddard and colleagues (2001) found that trust makes schools better places for students to learn; the greater the trust, the greater the student achievement.

> I decided to stay at this school because I am an athlete and I am a part of several extracurricular organizations at the school. If I were to leave, I would have let down my teammates. I also did not want to start all over again as far as getting to know a new school and new people. In a way, since people feel this is a bad school I wanted to let them know that I can do something good here. There are some people at this school that can do good things. However, I do know some people will think that I cannot do much because I attended River High, and think other students can do more because they attended better schools. —*Ruth*, River High School

> No matter what the problems are at River High I would not leave it for anything in the world. I love my school. I wanted to get to attend this school since I was in elementary school. I have always lived down the street from the school. When I was going to elementary school, I would look from through the window from the bus at River High and say, "One day I am going there." When the opportunity came to choose another school, I said, "Forget it; I am where I want to be." —*Omar*, River High School

Another predominant view among the participants was that graduating from an academically unacceptable school would translate into future success as an adult. Student participants felt if all variables were the same, students would fare better in life if they graduated from their present school rather than a higher performing school. The participants believed that their experiences at Lake High and River High mirrored those that are common in the "real world." Thus, it was assumed by the participants in this study that attending these socially challenging schools would make them better equipped for the perils of life. Furthermore, the totality of their experience, as evinced by their responses, fosters the development of vital character traits such as resilience, persistence, and tenacity. This is of particular importance in light of Bonner's (1997) study, which found that African American students emerge into the adult world confused about their identity, and they have problems relating to black and nonblack populations. This particular group of students may not have such problems because they may have observed or endured similar life lessons in high school.

> I decided to stay at this school because I feel comfortable here. A part of learning is opening your mind. You can't accomplish that by feeling uncomfortable. I think that I will probably come out as a better student than somebody who came out of a better [performing] school, just because I had extra problems to deal with and if we made the same score, and I went through a little bit more, it will make me a better person overall. —Warren, River High School

> One reason I decided to stay at this school is that it does not matter what I school go to; I can still get a good education if I stay focused and listen to my teachers. I also feel very comfortable here at River High. I want to also prove people wrong who would say it's not a good school. I really feel that I will be more successful graduating from here because I am dealing with situations that occur in the real world and that will help prepare me for real life. —Xana, River High School

CONCLUSIONS

It is unlikely that the designers of accountability systems can fathom the conditions present in academically unacceptable schools. For the average student, such conditions are insurmountable and subsequently inhibit their ability to achieve academically in challenging subjects like mathematics. Fortunately, the students in this study are among a cadre of exceptional students who are able to persevere in spite of being placed in undesirable conditions. They exhibit an uncanny resilience that seems to immunize them from the perils associated with academically unacceptable schools.

Educators and those who aspire to improve low-performing schools must take heed of the advice of those students who have experienced success in unacceptable schools. Although it may seem a cliché, unacceptable schools need good mathematics teachers: yet it will take a monumental shift in educational policy to attract good mathematics teachers to poor-performing schools. Moreover, such transformation calls for a redistribution of funds that provide worthwhile incentives for teachers to work in low-performing schools and meaningful professional development to help teachers engage in instructional practices that lead to high achievement and increased efficacy among inner-city high school students.

Metaphorically, remedies such as the above would require an "act of Congress." Unfortunately, if you consider Congress's track record on educational reform, that may not even be a wise decision. As a result of the congressionally approved No Child Left Behind Act, low-performing schools are bemoaned with defamatory labels. Judiciously, the act offers students the chance to switch schools, but preliminary results show that large numbers of students have an unwavering commitment to their schools. Furthermore, high schools have evolved into social phenomena that promote school pride; that same school pride evokes a sense of school citizenship that is unlikely to succumb to the lure of a better performing school—which in many ways negates the concept of school choice.

Nonetheless, few solutions include the suggestions of students who actually succeed while enduring troubling circumstances. If input from successful mathematics students is consistently ignored, it is likely that the current achievement gap will persist. Consequently, a generation of underserved African Americans from inner-city schools may become disenfranchised—with limited means to prosper.

REFERENCES

Bauman, K. J. (1998). Direct measures of poverty as indicators of economic need: Evidence from the Survey of Income and Program Participation. Working Paper Series. Washington, DC: Population Division, U.S. Census Bureau, 43.

Bonner, W. W. (1997). Black male perspectives of counseling on a predominately white university campus. *Journal of Black Studies* 27(3), 395–408.

Du Bois, W. E. B. (1903). The talented tenth. In *The Negro problem: a series of articles by representative American Negroes of today* (pp. 33–75). New York: James Pott & Co. Retrieved July 25, 2004, from http://douglass archives.org/dubo_b05.htm

Finn, J. (1989). Withdrawing from school. *Review of Educational Research* 59: 117–43.

Finn, J. D., and Cox, D. (1992, Spring). Participation and withdrawal among fourth-grade pupils. *American Educational Research Journal*, 29(1), 141–62.

Goddard, R. D., Tschannen-Moran, M., and Hoy, W. K. (2001). A multilevel examination of the distribution and effects of teacher trust in students and parents in urban elementary schools. *The Elementary School Journal* 102, 3–17.

Horn, C. (2003). High stakes testing and students: Stopping or perpetuating a cycle of failure? *Theory into Practice* 42(1), 30–43.

Jipguep, M., and Sanders-Phillips, K. (2003). The context of violence for children of color: Violence in the community and in the media. *The Journal of Negro Education* 72(4), 379–89.

Kohn, A. (2000). Burnt at the high stakes. *Journal of Teacher Education* 51(4), 315–27.

Ladson-Billings, G. (1998). Teaching in dangerous times: Culturally relevant approaches to teacher assessment. *The Journal of Negro Education* 67(3), 255–67.

Louisiana Department of Education. (2003). Criterion-referenced test State Subgroup Classification Report. Retrieved July 10, 2005, from www .louisianaschools.net/lde/uploads/3520.pdf

Marshall, C., and Rossmann, G. (1995). *Designing qualitative research*. Thousand Oaks, CA: Sage Publications.

Martin, D. (2000). *Mathematics success and failure among African American youth*. Mahwah, NJ: Lawrence Erlbaum Associates.

Maton, K., Hrabowski, F., and Grief, G. (1998). Preparing the way: A qualitative study of high-achieving African American males and the role of the family. *American Journal of Community Psychology* 26(4), 639–69.

Merriam, S. (1998). *Qualitative research and case study applications in education*. San Francisco: Jossey-Bass Publishers.

Milner, H. R. (2002). Affective and social issues among high achieving African American students: Recommendations for teachers and teacher education. *Action in Teacher Education* 24(1), 81–89.

Seidman, I. (1998). *Interviewing as qualitative research*. New York: Teachers College Press.

Sireci, S., Deleon, B., and Washington, E. (2002). Improving teachers of minority students' attitudes towards and knowledge of standardized tests. *Academic Exchange Quarterly* 6(1), 162–68.

Sullivan, P. (2004). Beyond black white and brown. *The Nation*. Retrieved March 30, 2005, from www.thenation.com/doc.mhtml?i=20040503&c=6&s=forum

Tucker, C., Herman, K., Pederson, T., Vogel, D., and Reinke, W. (2000). Student generated solutions to enhance the academic success of African-American youth. *Child Study Journal* 30(3), 205–17.

CHAPTER 11

Counseling African American Girls in a White School Setting

The Empowerment Groups for Academic Success Model

TWANA HILTON-PITRE

Every child wants to believe in himself or herself as a successful person; every youngster wants to be liked and respected; and youngsters want life to be just.

—Stevenson, 1992, p. 3

INTRODUCTION

African American adolescents deal with many complex challenges in predominately white middle-school settings. African American students may be faced with the challenges of not being accepted by their peers and teachers when they first enter a predominately white school system (James, 1997). In addition, adolescence is a period of transition and how adolescents negotiate this formative period can have lifelong consequences (Guttman and Midgley, 2000). According to the Carnegie Council on Adolescent Development (1995), nearly half of America's adolescents are at high or moderate risk of seriously "damaging their life chances"—referring to inappropriate adolescent decisions that may affect both short-term and long-term academic, career, and personal needs.

Group intervention strategies can be used to address these needs of African American students. Holcomb-McCoy (2005) stated that "by encouraging more flexible group interventions to meet students' needs, school counselors will be able to address the 'root' of problems rather than the symptoms" (p. 182). The Empowerment Groups for Academic Success (EGAS) model has recently been used by school counselors to positively impact the behavior and academic achievement of urban

African American girls (Bemak, Chi-Ying, and Siroskey-Sabdo, 2005; Butler and Bunch, 2005; Holcomb-McCoy, 2005; Lee, 2005). In expanding applications, my research provides data regarding the applicability of the EGAS model in a nonurban setting with African American female adolescents in a predominantly white school setting.

The American School Counselor Association (ASCA) promotes a national model encouraging school counselors to take action to ensure that students of culturally diverse backgrounds have access to appropriate services and opportunities that promote the maximum development of the individual (ASCA, 2003). This is supported in the No Child Left Behind Act (Paige, 2001), which indicates that it is the responsibility of schools to provide resources or supplemental services for students who are lagging behind developmentally, academically, and socially. The goal is to specifically target the achievement gap between disadvantaged minority students and their peers. The school counselor's responsibility is to be accountable for demonstrating how the school-counseling program contributes to the commitment of the school agenda in closing the gap (Garza, 2004).

ASCA (2003) presented the ASCA National Model to guide development and implementation of school-counseling programs through a framework designed to promote every student's development in academic, career, and personal-social domains (Galassi and Akos, 2004). School counselors are being urged to take leadership roles in educational reform aimed at reducing the barriers to academic achievement for minority students (ASCA, 2003; Bemak, 2002; Butler, 2003; Taylor and Adelman, 2000). Culturally responsive guidance programs in schools should be based on two assumptions: (1) All young people can learn and want to learn; and (2) Cultural differences are real and cannot be ignored (Bryan, 2005).

Culturally responsive counseling practice requires an ethic of caring and understanding in an effort to build bridges among children whose cultures and backgrounds do not necessarily mirror the cultural dictates of mainstream American society (Day-Vines, 2003). Recognition of complex issues related to race, culture, and class will better position counselors to deliver more effective counseling services. Often, the culture of the home and the culture of the school remain unsynchronized for minority students (Patton and Day-Vines, 2003). Patton and

Day-Vines documented in their research that culturally responsive school-counseling programs should accommodate the emerging demands of children from culturally distinct groups.

Culturally responsive school counselors recognize students' culturally derived behaviors and interpret those behaviors appropriately, without construing such behavior as strange or inferring pathology in a student (Ransom, 2003). They demonstrate comfort exploring and processing the specific and unique manner in which culture may impact a student's values, viewpoints, and interpretation of stimuli. Culturally responsive school counselors who recognize potential dilemmas are in a better position to provide support and encourage counseling interventions for minority adolescents (Lee, 2001).

EMPOWERMENT GROUPS FOR ACADEMIC SUCCESS

Empowerment Groups for Academic Success (EGAS) is an innovative group-counseling approach that takes into account the influence of social, psychological, and environmental factors on academic performance for inner-city youth (Bemak et al., 2005). The EGAS approach was developed with the belief that structured group interventions that narrowly target only one of many problem areas for students of high risk and approaches that do not allow ownership for the group fall short of dealing with the complexity of problems that many urban adolescents face. Lee (2005) explained that counselors do not empower the people with whom they work: "Empowerment is an internal developmental process in which a person discovers how power operates in his or her life and then takes reasonable steps to seize upon personal power and channel it in constructive ways" (393). Lee adds that counselors provide the facilitative conditions that allow people to discover the internal resources to move their lives in positive directions. The EGAS approach incorporates attention to the concerns of group members, allowing them to determine the agenda and to establish and maintain many of the norms for behavior in and beyond the group (Bemak et al., 2005).

The EGAS approach to group counseling is unique in its emphasis on empowerment through group process, moving away from psycho-educational and traditional structured groups filled with exercises and activities planned by the facilitator (Lee, 2005). Lee suggests that a crucial difference between the EGAS approach and other groups is the responsibility placed upon the group members to establish their own agenda that centers on the goals of the group. EGAS is based on a core belief that facilitators should not "control" groups so that true empowerment results in members having an actual say in how a group is run. Bemak and colleagues (2005) noted that this is most effectively accomplished through an unstructured process with a group that has clearly defined goals.

The EGAS model, however, uses some of the traditional strategies and structures from the group counseling movement in the 1960s and 1970s, such as having a cofacilitator, establishing a set number of meetings, setting individual objectives, and building group cohesion and support (Johnson and Johnson, 2005). Moreover, Johnson and Johnson argue that the model goes beyond the traditional approach by building in a multicultural approach that is sensitive to the environmental elements that impact students living in urban settings.

PURPOSE OF THE STUDY

The purpose of this study was to examine the experiences of African American adolescent girls in a predominately white middle-school setting who participated in the EGAS model.

The EGAS model has had a positive impact on urban African American girls; however, concern exists that the EGAS model lacks credible research to provide the basis for application in different school settings (Butler and Bunch, 2005). Therefore, this study utilized the EGAS model as a framework in a non-urban, predominately white middle-school setting to capture the experiences of this model on minority adolescents from varied settings.

This study contributed to the potential for expanded applications by exploring the following research questions:

1. What are the experiences of minority adolescent girls who participate in the EGAS model in a predominately white middle-school setting?

2. What are the participants' perceptions of the outcome of the EGAS model?
3. What are the participants' perceptions of their experiences during group sessions?
4. How does the EGAS model impact the participants' personal, social, academic, and career needs?
5. How does this model work in a predominately white suburban setting with minority adolescents?

METHODS

This study examines the phenomenological experience of African American adolescents who participated in EGAS within a white middle-school setting. A constructivist approach was taken as the center of applicability of the EGAS model with minority adolescents in a suburban setting. The constructivism paradigm fits with a need for: (1) enhancing awareness of the EGAS model and its applicability to diverse backgrounds (people-students) and locations (schools) and (2) understanding how school counselors may be able to address the personal, social, academic, and career needs of students of color in predominately white middle-school settings. For the purpose of this study, the eight-week group-counseling sessions were held in a classroom with natural light illuminating multiple windows. The chairs were arranged in a circular formation to allow for face-to-face interactions during the EGAS process. The group met once a week for 45 minutes during elective classes. The group leaders were two African American female facilitators, with the school counselor being the lead facilitator and the researcher as cofacilitator. The first group session began in October 2006 and included eight weekly group counseling sessions.

Sample Selection

This study was conducted at a suburban middle school located in a southern, Gulf Coast city. Administrators of this suburban middle school were highly interested in committing to new interventions that would aid in the contribution of helping African American female adolescents achieve. This school is one of the highest performing middle schools in the state, providing educational programs to students in grades five through eight. The school's mission is to focus on teamwork, a positive learning environment, and meaningful activities to ensure student success. This middle school has approximately 689 students, and the overall student body is comprised primarily of five major ethnic groups: whites (79 percent), African Americans (15 percent), Hispanics (4 percent), Asians (1 percent), and American Indians (1 percent). The percentage of families who receive free and reduced lunch is 9 percent.

For the benefit of this study, purposeful sampling within the identified setting was the method of choice. The target population for this study was eight minority adolescent eighth-grade girls identified by the school counselor. *Minority* refers to four major racial and ethnic groups: African American, American Indian and Alaska natives, Asian and Pacific Islanders, and Hispanics (Polland and O'Hare, 1999). In this study, girls from all four minority groups had the potential to participate or be selected to participate.

Data Collection

Following each group session the researcher kept field notes and the participants were asked to write self-reflections of their group experience in a diary. Given the age range of the participants, three questions were prewritten in each student's weekly diary. This helped with the issue of having a blank page at the end of each session. The students were given five minutes at the end of each session to write in their diaries. The diaries were collected by the researcher at the end of each group session. At the end of the eight-week session, the researcher conducted individual, semi-structured, face-to-face interviews. A Student Interview Form with eight open-ended questions was read aloud and available to each participant before responding to each question.

Interviews were the primary instruments for data collection. The researcher conducted face-to-face interviews with all participants of the group. These interviews lasted approximately 15 to 45 minutes. Pseudonyms were developed to protect the identity and location of the participants. During the interview, the researcher used an audio recorder and notepad to accurately record the participants' verbal and nonverbal responses as well as interviewer observations.

Participant Weekly Diary

1. MY THOUGHTS . . .
2. What was most helpful for you this session?
3. Is there anything else you would like to share?

Student Interview Form

1. Please tell me about yourself.
2. Please tell me about your experiences during the EGAS group sessions.
3. What helped you the most during the group sessions?
4. If you were facilitator, what might you change or how would the group sessions look?
5. How have you changed as a result of participating in this group?
6. How do you think your peers changed?
7. Do you think groups like this should continue to be offered and why or why not?
8. Is there anything else you would like to share with me?

Data Analysis

Interviews with the participants were transcribed immediately after the face-to-face interviews to capture the fresh perspectives of the participants. During the transcription process, interviews were read and compared with the audiotapes by the researcher. Re-reading these transcriptions allowed the researcher to accurately record the voices as well as "get a sense of what the text is about" (Darlington and Scott, 2002, p. 144). This process ensured the researcher of her "conscious effort to stay in the words of the participants, without theorizing or analyzing based on the researcher's experiences and notions, and to focus on the phenomenon that appeared" (Ray, 2001, p. 40).

The interview transcripts, diaries, and observational notes were coded using an inductive approach appropriate to a phenomenological study (Willig, 2001). The coding process was informed by the theory and literature associated with the EGAS model, but a general inductive coding process followed the steps of reading the participants' materials, coding themes, and then clustering these themes into major themes (Willig, 2001). This procedure was performed with data of each participant (within-case analysis) and then all the participant themes were compared and contrasted (cross-case analysis). This allowed for the essence of the students' experience with EGAS to emerge.

Verification

Weekly field notes were kept to contribute to the credibility and dependability of the study. In the context of contributing to trustworthiness, the research participants' personal diaries assisted in reducing potential negative influences on credible data. The researcher provided detailed documentation, transcripts, and notes for informed colleagues to replicate the study.

Member checking was used to ensure that participant "voices" were accurately reflected in the study. Peer reviews were used to examine research chapters, proposals, and research instruments for corrections. The researcher utilized the expertise of colleagues and peers to examine and analyze the procedures, texts, and references.

In this study, triangulation of the data was achieved by analyzing the diaries of participants, the researcher's field notes, and individual participant interviews. Additionally, the use of both written and oral communications enhanced the data-collection process as they allowed individuals with different communication preferences and strengths to fully participate in the study. This process ensured the credibility of the research study.

Findings

The eighth-grade adolescents in this study were all African American females of diverse ages ranging from 11 to 15 years. Seven out of eight participants reported that they had changed in some aspects due to the participation in the EGAS model. All participants agreed that EGAS should continue to be offered. In the same way, participant experiences also varied to some extent. Personal, social, career, and academic development issues were evident and varied among participants. Personal, career, and social development issues were higher for most of the participants. Academic development issues were discussed, but not as frequently mentioned as the above development categories. Similarly, themes emerged through the use of the adolescents' weekly diaries, individual face-to-face interviews, and the researcher's field notes. The emergent themes include social support, racial relations, identity development, conflict resolution, and career preparation.

Social Support

African American students may be faced with the challenges of not being accepted by their peers and teachers when they first enter a predominately white school system (James, 1997). Many participants in this study commented, "I got to socialize and express thoughts and feelings with others. Group sessions really helped to make us a closer group." Research has demonstrated that adolescents perform better academically, have more achievement-oriented goals, and think more about their future when they have access to mentors (Zirkel, 2002). Some participants remarked, "The sessions taught us to be better people and choose more goals in life. [They] also helped to have two positive African American female counselors/role models during the EGAS group sessions."

Participants indicated, "Even something we wouldn't normally talk about, somebody else might bring it up and it made you think . . . I have a problem with that, too." Groups can provide the support, understanding, acceptance, companionship, and opportunity for growth that these students may need (Sue and Sue, 1999). In this study, participants discussed their appreciation for being able to talk to people their age and race with similar experiences or problems. Ford (1997) suggested that the opportunity to speak with other students who share their concerns may help minority students become more comfortable with "being different." Group counseling offers understanding and support, which promotes students' willingness to explore problems and assets they have with the group (Corey, 2004). Some participants were angry and socially withdrawn prior to participating in EGAS group sessions.

Those particular participants actually gained more friendships during the EGAS group and their attitude toward others became positive.

Racial Relations

"Adolescents' struggle for independence and identity often makes them 'hypersensitive' to circumstances where they feel others are asserting power over them or simply talking about them" (Lambie, 2004, p. 269). As a result, this period of the child's life is when some students come into contact with issues of racial relations (Ransom, 2003). In this study, most participants talked about various school race issues. These issues included comments about the lack of black history, prejudice, and discrimination. James (1997) explained that a lack of acceptance might occur because of misunderstanding based on the differences in language and patterns of speech. Many participants in this study complained about being teased by white students for the way they talk.

Many patterns of racial group relations in our schools are based on the ways that members of a given racial group have been included or excluded within American society (McLemore and Romo, 1998).

Identity Development

A large part of early adolescents' social-emotional growth is tied to identity development (Lambie, 2004). Classic Ericksonian psychosocial theory described early adolescence as a drive toward industry and identity versus inferiority and role confusion (Cobb, 2001). Accordingly, questions like "What am I like?" "Who am I?" "How good am I?" are deemed of higher importance by adolescents (Hansen and Maynard, 1973). Adolescents are trying to discover their own identities and yet realize that they are a part of a social group (Cobb, 2001). Members of the EGAS group talked about the importance of being able to talk to other African American eighth-grade girls. Additional comments included, "It was nice to have an all-black group, because everything we do is white." "Everybody was black and looked like me." White and Parham (1990) defined identity as "the adoption of certain personal attitudes, feelings, characteristics, and behaviors and the identification with a large group of people who share those characteristics" (p. 42). One's identity is paramount in understanding self. Minority adolescents are looking for the answers for who they are in terms of their race.

Conflict Resolution

Adolescence is a period in which new situations, new settings, and new demands are constantly being encountered, and yet the adolescent may be ill equipped with the knowledge or skills necessary to effectively respond to these confrontations (Tyszkowa, 1990). During the EGAS group sessions, all participants wanted to learn ways of dealing with discrimination, teasing, prejudice, and racism. As a result of EGAS, members learned how to handle situations or disputes in a mature way. A participant commented, "It was helpful to learn how to deal with racial problems . . . I think I got better, 'cause normally, I would just lash out at people."

Group counseling allows adolescents the chance to pool their expertise so that they may jointly strategize ways to resolve problems and cope with negative situations (Schmidt, 2003).

Career Preparation

This study indicates that suburban African American female adolescents in a predominately white middle-school setting may also have limited knowledge of themselves and their career interests. Participants commented, "The EGAS sessions taught me to be a better person and choose more goals in life. I enjoyed talking about career goals." One member discussed, "I am struggling with what career choices I want to make, but the career choices information packet helped a lot."

Lack of career planning may further limit African American student perceptions and knowledge of available job opportunities. Without solid career-planning programs at the middle-school level, many students will make poor educational and career choices in high school (Sears, 1995). One EGAS participant mentioned, "I enjoyed talking about careers. I learned I can be anything I want to be and go to college instead of just be a beautician."

DISCUSSION

In this section, the findings of this study indicate recommendations for middle-school counselors who work with African American adolescents. Many of these recommendations come directly from the African American female adolescents in the study; others are findings based upon EGAS perceptions, review of literature, and the breadth of information collected.

Recommendations for Middle-School Counselors

Intervention

While the number of minority students in public school is increasing, African American female students' personal, social, career, and academic needs are still not being met. Their needs, as well as cultural diversity, should be addressed within comprehensive school counseling programs. It is important to promote cultural diversity in school-counseling interventions.

The EGAS model is a good intervention to implement in a diverse urban-school setting, in addition to the current findings of the application in a predominately white suburban setting. If middle-school counselors plan to better serve African American students and their needs, it is likely that counselors will need to revise their theories, techniques, and interventions.

Some of the recommendations made to assist middle-school counselors who work with minority adolescents include:

1. Partner with other middle-school counselors who are actively engaged in conducting group counseling in urban and suburban public schools. Introduce the EGAS model.
2. Educate and partner with other middle-school counselors in local school districts about the importance of addressing needs of all adolescents. Introduce the EGAS model.
3. Educate and partner with college and university counseling programs about the lessons learned in the use of the EGAS model.
4. Broaden thinking of teachers and administrators regarding the importance of time allotment for group counseling intervention

techniques such as EGAS and its potential impact for minority adolescents.

Student Advocacy

Lee (1998) defined advocacy as "the process or act of arguing or pleading for a cause or proposal" (p. 8). The EGAS group sessions during this study exposed some of the challenges African American female adolescents are faced with in a predominately white middle-school setting. After conducting EGAS group-counseling sessions, middle-school counselors are given ideas as to what issues may need to be addressed individually or schoolwide. School counselors, as advocates for students, may have a huge impact on individual student achievement and school climate. Recommendations to assist school-counseling advocacy for minority adolescents include:

1. Conduct EGAS group-counseling sessions to assist with identifying potential academic, career, personal, and social advocacy needs.
2. Educate teachers and administrators about the importance of having a multicultural school climate.
3. Conduct in-service workshops for teachers and administrators (e.g., multicultural education, conflict resolution, peer support groups, institutional barriers, and cultural insensitivities).
4. Develop mentoring programs for minority students; help students build support-advocacy networks with teachers within the school.

Career Preparation

The goal is to meet the needs of career development for all students; however, this study has shown that some African American female adolescents do not have a solid foundation in the area of career planning. Without a career plan, minority students tend to make poor educational and career choices. Recommendations include:

1. Conduct EGAS sessions to gain ideas of the level of career preparation individual members have.

2. Educate and expand students' thinking about goals and careers during EGAS sessions.
3. Develop a mentoring program to build career interest. Students may be able to shadow a career professional for a day.
4. Implement a career fair during school time and include guest speakers of various professions and cultures represented as role models.
5. Partner with teachers and administrators to plan and implement career-oriented mini-lessons.

Research conducted by Bemak and colleagues (2005) notes the impact of the EGAS approach on seven African American high school girls in an urban-school setting. Based upon the self-reports supplied by the seven girls, some participants reported an improvement in academic achievement and in their behavior after EGAS. Similarly, this current study also included self-reports of participants' improvement of behavior and increased homework completion.

Some of the key factors that EGAS addressed were the personal, social, academic, and career development needs of minority adolescents. More important, the group offered freedom of speech and expression of feelings due to the unique EGAS model, which allows the adolescent participants to have ownership of the group's agenda based on the defined goals for the group. In this study, minority adolescents seemed to thoroughly enjoy having a certain degree of control and an actual say in how a group is run. As a result of the EGAS model, true empowerment emerged.

LESSONS LEARNED

This study has expanded the applicability of the EGAS model in several ways. It can also be used: (1) in a suburban versus urban public school; (2) in a predominately white school versus diverse school populations; and (3) with middle school minority adolescents vs. high school adolescents.

Holcomb-McCoy (2005) articulates that empowerment groups for African American girls should be led by at least one African American female.

An African American female counselor who has an understanding of Afrocentric or black feminism would be the most effective leader [for] an empowerment group for African American girls because she can act as a role model and can offer emotional support for the girls in identifying and responding to racism. (p. 392)

This study utilized two African American female facilitators during the EGAS process. Participants acknowledged their appreciation for having two positive African American role models, which also helped with emotional support and being able to relate to the participants during times of disclosure about racism and discrimination. Participants reported that their comfort level to disclose various issues was high due to the fact that the facilitators looked like them. In my observations, this added richness and a level of understanding for everyone, including the facilitators.

The overarching research question for this study dealt with the experiences of African American adolescent girls who participated in the EGAS model in a predominately white middle-school setting. EGAS appears to be an effective intervention for addressing the various needs of African American female adolescents. The EGAS model satisfies the requirements emphasized by the ASCA national model (2003), which addresses the importance of personal, social, academic, and career development for all students within a comprehensive school-counseling program.

The commonalities of the participants' experiences were combinations of the following: (1) social support, (2) dealing with racial relations, (3) identity development, (4) learning conflict resolution, and (5) career preparation. In this study, the EGAS approach was powerful in allowing the minority adolescents to address personal, social, academic, and career concerns during weekly sessions. Participants' self-reported improvements in their behaviors, attitudes, friendships, test-taking skills, homework, and career knowledge. The group sessions gave individual participants a sense of identity and belonging. During group sessions, members were able to release anger and other strong feelings and learned how to tactfully resolve conflicts.

Of central importance is the need for careful attention to interventions that address the personal, social, career, and academic needs of all students. EGAS is a viable start. The EGAS model and the themes that emerged during this study were interrelated. The themes began to over-lap and influence each other. A unique quality of EGAS is that it en-abled African American female adolescents to be instrumental in one another's growth in the areas of identity development, career prepara-tion, conflict resolution, racial relations, and social support. Minority adolescents struggle with high rates of school failure, dropouts, vio-lence, racism, drug use, teenage pregnancy, parent neglect, and low teacher expectations. EGAS group counseling can be a supportive en-vironment and an opportunity to explore these issues. The approach also allows African American female adolescents to experience a true sense of empowerment and control over their destinies.

REFERENCES

Akos, P., and Galassi, J. (2004). Gender and race as factors in psychosocial ad-justment to middle and high school. *The Journal of Educational Research* 98(2), 102–8.

American School Counselor Association. (2003). *The ASCA national model: A framework for school counseling programs*. Alexandria, VA: Author.

Bemak, F. (2002). Paradigms for future counseling programs. In C. D. John-son and S. K. Johnson (Eds.), *Building stronger school counseling pro-grams: Bringing futuristic approaches into the present* (pp. 37–49). Greens-boro, NC: ERIC Counseling & Student Services Clearinghouse.

Bemak, F., Chi-Ying, R., and Siroskey-Sabdo, L. (2005). Empowerment groups for academic success: An innovative approach to prevent high school failure for at-risk, urban African Americans. *Professional School Counseling* 5, 377–89.

Bryan, J. (2005). Fostering educational resilience and achievement in urban schools through school-family-community partnerships. *Professional School Counseling* 8, 219–27.

Butler, S. K. (2003). Helping urban African American high school students excel academically: The roles of school counselors. *High School Journal* 87, 51–57.

Butler, S. K., and Bunch, L. K. (2005). Response to EGAS: An innovative ap-proach to prevent high school failure for at-risk, urban African American girls. *Professional School Counseling* 5, 395–97.

Carnegie Council on Adolescent Development. (1995). *Great transitions: Preparing adolescents for the new century*. New York: Carnegie.

Cobb, N. (2001). *Adolescence: Continuity, change, and diversity* (4th ed.). Mountain View, CA: Mayfield.

Corey, G. F. (2004). *Theory and practice of group counseling*. Monterey, CA: Brooks/Cole.

Darlington, Y., and Scott, D. (2002). *Qualitative research in practice: Stories from the field*. Philadelphia: Open University Press.

Day-Vines, N. (2003). Counseling African American adolescents: The impact of race, cultural, and middle class status. *Professional School Counseling 7*, 40–52.

Ford, D. (1997). Counseling middle-class African Americans. In C. Lee (Ed.), *Multicultural issues in counseling: New approaches to diversity* (2nd ed., pp. 81–107). Alexandria, VA: American Counseling Association.

Garza, Y. (2004). Effects of culturally responsive child-centered play therapy compared to curriculum-based small group counseling with elementary-age Hispanic children experiencing externalizing and internalizing behavior problems: A preliminary study. Unpublished doctoral dissertation, University of North Texas.

Guttman, L., and Midgley, C. (2000). The role of protective factors in supporting the academic achievement of poor African American students during middle school transition. *Journal of Youth and Adolescence 29*, 223–48.

Hansen, J. C., and Maynard, P. E. (1973). *Youth: Self-concept and behavior*. Columbus, OH: Charles E. Merrill.

Holcomb-McCoy, C. D. (2005). Empowerment groups for urban African American girls: A response. *Professional School Counseling 5*, 390–92.

James, D. C. S. (1997). Psychosocial risks of immigrant students. *The Education Digest 63*, 51–53.

Johnson, S. K., and Johnson, C. D. (2005). Group counseling: Beyond the traditional. *Professional School Counseling 8*(5), 399–400.

Lambie, G. W. (2004). Motivational enhancement therapy: A tool for professional school counselors working with adolescents. *Professional School Counseling 7*, 267–76.

Lee, C. (1998). Counselors as agents of social change. In C. Lee and G. R. Waltz (Eds.), *Social action: A mandate for counselors* (pp. 3–16). Alexandria, VA: American Counseling Association.

Lee, C. G. (2001). Culturally responsive school counselors and programs: Addressing the needs of all students. *Professional School Counseling 4*, 257–61.

Lee, C. G. (2005). A reaction to EGAS: An important new approach to African American youth empowerment. *Professional School Counseling 8*, 393–94.

McLemore, S. D., and Romo, H. D. (1998). *Racial and ethnic relations in America* (5th ed.). Boston: Allyn & Bacon.

Paige, R. (2001). *No child left behind act: A new era*. U.S. Secretary of Education. Retrieved October 6, 2004, from www.ed.gov/nclb/overview/intro/index.html

Patton, J., and Day-Vines, N. (2003). *Strategies to guide the training of special and general education teachers*. Williamsburg, VA: College of William and Mary, School of Education.

Polland, K., and O'Hare, W. (1999). America's racial and ethnic minorities. *Population Bulletin* 54(3), 3–20.

Ransom, D. (2003). Race/ethnicity and social class: The impact on the role of middle school counselors in a diverse school environment. Unpublished doctoral dissertation, George Mason, Virginia.

Ray, R. (2001). The experiences of high school teachers with a zero tolerance for fighting policy. Unpublished doctoral dissertation, Colorado State University, Fort Collins.

Schmidt, E. (2003). A program design model for promoting social and emotional health through group counseling with middle school students. Unpublished doctoral dissertation, Rutgers, State University of New Jersey; New Brunswick.

Sears, S. (1995). Career and educational planning in the middle level school. *NASSP Bulletin* 79(570), 36–42.

Stevenson, C. (1992). *Teaching ten to fourteen year olds*. White Plains, NY: Longman.

Sue, D., and Sue, D. (1999). *Counseling the culturally different: Theory and practice* (3rd ed.). New York: John Wiley & Sons.

Taylor, L., and Adelman, H. S. (2000). Connecting schools, families, and communities. *Professional School Counseling* 3, 298–307.

Tyszkowa, M. (1990). Difficult school situations and stress resistance. In H. Bosma and S. Jackson (Eds.), *Coping and self-concept in adolescence* (pp. 189–201). New York: Springer-Verlag Berlin Heidelberg.

White, J. L., and Parham, T. A. (1990). *The psychology of blacks: An African American perspective* (2nd ed.). Englewood Cliffs, NJ: Prentice Hall.

Willig, C. (2001). *Introducing qualitative research in psychology: Adventures in theory and method*. Buckingham, PA: Open University Press.

Zirkel, S. (2002). Is there a place for me? Role models and academic identity among white students and students of color. *Teachers College Record* 2, 357–416.

About the Editors and Contributors

THE EDITORS

Abul Pitre is the former Carter G. Woodson Professor of Education at Edinboro University of Pennsylvania. Currently he is an associate professor of educational leadership at Fayetteville State University where he teaches doctoral courses in educational leadership. Dr. Pitre is the author of several articles and books. Most notable is his work on the educational philosophy of Elijah Muhammad.

Esrom Pitre is an associate principal at Donaldsonville High School. His areas of research are African American males in special education and multicultural education with a focus on racial issues as it relates to African American students.

Twana Hilton-Pitre is the director of field experiences at Louisiana State University, Shreveport. Her areas of expertise include counseling, multicultural education, and elementary education.

Ruth Ray is the department chair at Louisiana State University, Shreveport, where she teaches courses in educational leadership. Her major research interest is the impact of zero tolerance policy on African American students.

THE CONTRIBUTORS

Na'im Akbar is one of the world's preeminent African American psychologists and pioneer in the development of an African-centered approach to modern psychology. His books and articles exploring the personality of development of African Americans have led to numerous network television appearances, including *Phil Donahue*, *Oprah Winfrey*, *Geraldo*, and *Tony Brown's Journal*. He retired from Florida State University in 2008 after twenty-eight years on the psychology faculty. He is currently president and CEO of his private consulting and publishing company, Mind Productions & Associates, in Tallahassee, Florida.

Michelle Barconey is currently teaching in the Recovery School District in New Orleans, Louisiana. She obtained a master's of arts in teaching in urban schools in 2001 from Southern University New Orleans. While at SUNO, she completed a capstone titled *The Narrative Experiences of African American Males in Urban High Schools*.

Frank Cook is a retired professor of educational leadership from Southern University where he specialized in social studies education and educational leadership. Currently Dr. Cook is involved with community projects that are related to the education of African American students.

Terence Hicks is the chairperson and associate professor of research in the Department of Educational Leadership at Fayetteville State University, in North Carolina. Dr. Hicks is a noteworthy researcher who has been cited in the 2007 *Research Alert Yearbook*, *USA Today*, *Detroit News*, *Fayetteville Observer*, and on several university websites. To date, his research has been cited by over sixty combined national and international researchers and universities. Most recently, his research on college students has been cited in the second edition of *Academic Advising: A Comprehensive Handbook*, and in a new book titled, *Encountering Faith in the Classroom: Turning Difficult Discussions into Constructive Engagement*.

Rodrick Jenkins is currently a doctoral student in the Department of Educational Theory, Policy, and Practice at Louisiana State University in Baton Rouge, Louisiana, where he is majoring in curriculum theory with a focus on social studies education. He also teaches "Methods and Materials in Secondary Social Studies" and "Middle School Social Studies Methods" at Southern University and A&M College in Baton Rouge, Louisiana. His research focuses on the educational thought of black people and the ideological foundation of the school structure and social studies curriculum.

Chance Lewis is an associate professor of urban education at Texas A&M University. Dr. Lewis has authored several journal articles and written two books. His most acclaimed book, *White Teachers/Diverse Classrooms*, coedited with Julie Landsman, has been widely read by educational scholars. Dr. Lewis has recently copublished a book titled: *The Dilemmas of Being an African American Male in the New Millennium: Solutions for Life Transformation*.

Carol D. McCree is an assistant professor in the Department of Educational Leadership at Southern University and A&M College in Baton Rouge, Louisiana. She presently teaches Fostering Community Support in Schools, Vision of Leadership: Issues, Trends, and Practices, and Administrative Internship to candidates preparing to become leaders in public schools. Dr. McCree is also the international program coordinator for the College of Education at Southern University. In this capacity she coordinates a partnership between Southern University and the public schools in Belize.

Shahid Muhammad received a master's degree in mathematics from Lincoln University and has served as the director of the Masters of Adult Education Developmental Studies Program at National Louis University. He served as head of the Mathematics Department at the Muhammad University in Chicago where he monitored and evaluated the entire mathematics program and developed curriculum. He has written and published several books. *How to Teach Math to Black Students* is considered a favorite among educators and scholars alike.

Peter Sheppard is an assistant professor of mathematics education at the University of Louisiana, Lafayette. His research interests include Mathematics Teacher Preparation, High-Achieving African American Mathematics Students, Diagnostic and Prescriptive Mathematics Teaching, and The Influence of Accountability Systems on Mathematics Teaching and Learning.

Luria Stubblefield is an associate professor of curriculum and instruction at Southern University. Dr. Stubblefield's research interests include increasing the number of African American students majoring in science education and African American issues in higher education.